6299 Tanglewood

Grand Blanc

Mich.

48439

Barbara

Schramm

HOW TO HELP YOUR CHILD GET THE MOST OUT OF SCHOOL

How to Help Your Child Get the Most Out of School

STELLA CHESS, M.D.

WITH JANE WHITBREAD

DOUBLEDAY & COMPANY, INC.

GARDEN CITY, NEW YORK

1974

Library of Congress Cataloging in Publication Data

Chess, Stella.
    How to help your child get the most out of school.

    1. Home and school. 2. Parent-teacher relationships. 3. Education
of children. I. Whitbread, Jane, joint author. II. Title.

LC225.C48   372
ISBN: 0-385-06746-1
Library of Congress Catalog Card Number: 74-1769

PREFACE

Children don't always get report cards these days, but parents worry more than ever, it seems, about how they are getting along in school. People have many different goals for themselves and their children, but almost all mothers and fathers consider schoolwork a pretty good gauge of children's future prospects.

How does Sally get along with her classmates? Teachers? Does she work hard? Pay attention? Is Josh enthusiastic about first grade? Is Pat learning to work by himself in third grade? Is Jim dependable? Quick? How does he compare with Peter, Paul, or Marianne?

Parents ask these questions about their children in school because they are the questions our society asks in judging doctors, lawyers, merchants, chiefs, writers, dancers, composers, plumbers, and painters.

When children do not do well—in fact, even when there are intimations that they might be headed for trouble—parents want to help. Often they do exactly the right thing. But, sometimes, with the best intentions, they create problems where none existed; make minor difficulties major; or overlook small problems that timely attention might have corrected easily.

Parents need guidance themselves to be able to judge their children's progress in school and give them the proper help when help is needed. *How to Help Your Child Get the Most Out of School* answers the questions that come up in children's formative preschool and elementary years.

What is early learning? What should parents teach? How can you best prepare your child for school? Do babies and toddlers in day care centers get a head start for school? When is day care dangerous? Can you teach little children too much, too soon? Do you know why you are a natural teacher? When should you "see the teacher"? How can you help the teacher help your child? How can the teacher help you? What does psychological testing tell? When is it misused? Can your helping hurt? Does the child who learns fast learn best? Doesn't competition make children work harder?

How to Help Your Child Get the Most Out of School tells how children learn, discusses the differences in normal learning rates and styles, identifies the common problems of the early years, and offers clear and simple advice to help parents solve them. It includes valuable material about where to go for diagnosis and treatment of learning difficulties.

The authors write both as experts and parents. Stella Chess is a child psychiatrist known around the world for her study (now in its eighteenth year) on temperamental differences in infants and their complex and subtle effects on development (The New York Study). Reviewing her career recently, she found that she had seen over two thousand children in private consultation and treatment and many thousands more in hospitals and children's centers. She is professor of pediatric psychiatry at New York University-Bellevue Medical School and supervises the psychiatric evaluation and treatment of children admitted to the pediatric clinic— a program in preventive psychiatry she developed.

Her work with troubled children and their families, and her experience as a parent give her a fine and tender appreciation of parents' concerns and children's needs. Jane Whitbread, a journalist who reports on child development and schools, met Dr. Chess when she interviewed her for a New York *Times Magazine* article on the effect of children's temperamental difference on parent-child relations and child development. The article led to Jane Whitbread's editorial work on *Your Child Is a Person*—a parents' guide based on the individuality study, and finally to their collaboration on this book.

The solid scientific wisdom in *How to Help Your Child Get the Most Out of School* is dispensed in family-sized prescriptions. The authors use their personal and professional experience, enriched with material gathered from discussions with pediatricians, psychiatrists, psychologists, teachers, and parents, and observation at many elementary and special school classes across the country.

—The Editors

ACKNOWLEDGMENTS

We would like to express our special appreciation to Mrs. Katrina de Hirsch for reading the entire manuscript and offering valuable critical suggestions for the chapter on dyslexia and other central language difficulties affecting learning, and to Dr. Alexander Thomas who has given us advice and support from the beginning.

We would also like to acknowledge the interested cooperation of school administrators, principals, guidance teachers, special education teachers, day care specialists, parents, and children whom we have interviewed and observed in action in the course of documenting the chapters in this book; particularly, Hilda Bakst, Judith Birsh, Sidney Blitz, Maureen Bradley, Dr. Dale Bryant, Caroline Church, Anita Dore, Melanie Dugan, Janet Faxon, Irene Gifford, Barbara Gauthier, Maria Gravel, Josephine Hartog, Minerva Jorn, Georgianna Khatib, Mary Jane Laidlaw, Dr. George P. Lane, Tracy MacGruer, R. Michael McNaught, Ann Macuk, Georgianna O'Connell, Elizabeth Pizzichemi, Edith Renna, Theresa Revans, Charlotte Schiff, Hannah Elizabeth Stebbins, Blanche Stein, Timothy Sugrue, Betty Terrall, Betty Vernon, Cynthia Webber, Carol Wolf, Billie Carrington Woodward, Margaret Wrigney, Jack Zuckerman.

Our special thanks to Mary Stefanich who typed the manuscript quickly, flawlessly, and beautifully.

The Authors

CONTENTS

xii *Contents*

LEARNING HOW TO HELP
YOUR CHILD IN SCHOOL

Are you a little anxious about how your children are getting along in school? Do you wonder whether there isn't something you should do about it? Are you unsure about how to help when you think help is needed?

If so, you are a typical American parent.

Almost all the parents I know—and they run into thousands—worry about school. With my husband, Dr. Alexander Thomas, and the late Dr. Herbert Birch, I have been following 231 children from infancy in an effort to find out how the temperamental qualities they were born with affect their development. During this New York longitudinal study's eighteen years, I have become well acquainted with the children's parents. I have noticed growing anxiety among them about their children's schoolwork. I have seen the same concern among the hundreds of parents who come to the pediatric clinic at New York City's great New York University-Bellevue Medical Center, where I organized and supervise the psychiatric service and train young psychiatrists. Moreover, the doctors and psychiatrists from

all over the country, whom I meet at meetings and conferences in my field, report the same problem.

Parents worry about their children more than they
used to, I feel, and principals and teachers worry more
about *them,* because anxious parents make very bad
vibrations in children.

It's one thing to be concerned parents, and quite another to be anxious hoverers. If you are concerned and
reasonably perceptive, you know when to relax and let
things alone and when to get in there and do something.
If you are an anxious hoverer, you do no good at all.
You cannot discriminate between good, bad, and indifferent behavior in children. That makes you indeci-
sive. You are never sure when to get advice or what to
do with it. This uncertainty makes for tension. You can't
enjoy your children and they feel it. They also pick up
your hesitancy and lack of assurance. It's contagious.
They become tense, self-conscious, and worried, too.
They worry about doing and saying the wrong thing.
Fearfulness interferes with their development. It's as if
they didn't dare try to learn. A child has to be willing
to take chances, make mistakes, and experiment in order to learn anything, whether it is how to walk, speak
French, or paint.

I hope I can help you understand enough about how
children learn, and how to recognize and respect your
own children's natural learning styles, so that you can
relax a bit, enjoy watching them progress, know when
and how to help, and how to keep from hurting.

However, this knowledge alone will not create the
confidence you need to guide them. You have to know,
also, what you want for them. Many parents don't.
Their anxiety and uncertainty come from several sources.
The many pendulum swings in child rearing and edu-

cational theory and practice that they have lived through have shaken their natural confidence in their roles.

In the early 1920s a handful of experimental schools began developing programs based on the innovative ideas of John Dewey and Sigmund Freud. This was child-centered education designed to meet the individual child's developing needs, interests, and abilities. The school offered the child a host of attractive choices. Teachers were not bosses, as much as informed guides. The theory was that a child's innate curiosity and delight in discovery would make him want to learn to read, write, and solve problems as eagerly as he had mastered block building, poster painting, and rhythms. To this end, the curriculum concentrated first on mastery of the immediate environment, moving gradually out into the community, and the national and international spheres.

On the assumption that young children learn as much from their senses and from direct experience as from books, tests, drills, and papers, all sorts of projects were created to enhance the content of the basic curriculum. Children built block cities with real lights in nursery school. They prepared and shared Roman banquets along with early Latin. Every effort was made to cherish children's fresh interest in life in the hope that it would stimulate lifelong exploration and mastery in whatever field they finally chose to work.

Just as this kind of education was beginning to have a broad influence on the American public school system it became a casualty of the space race that followed Sputnik in 1957. In the national hysteria to catch up with the Russians, many schools forgot about educating the whole child in favor of schooling to produce the most space engineers and electronics wizards fastest. Cramming was the method. Experimentation in education shifted from finding ways to develop effective, as well as educated human beings, to searching for ways to teach children higher mathematics at the earliest possible moment. Reports that babies have abstracting powers and can learn to read as they learn to talk set off an early-learning binge that has not yet subsided.

Even parents who believed that children learn best when allowed to set their own pace got shaky in the face of the college admissions crunch that developed in the late 1950s. Their anxiety about rising college applications, dwindling places, and tightening requirements left scars on the children, who are now young parents themselves. This is one source of parental confusion about whether to let children enjoy learning as a natural part of growing up, or push them to the "college of my choice" from kindergarten.

Another is the generalized tension, uncertainty, and anxiety abroad in the world. Today's children could become its victims. One way parents relieve their own anxiety is to push their children. Pushing hurts them in many ways.

Can you stop worrying about whether your two-year-old will make Harvard and the executive suite, and direct your attention, instead, to the spot where he is right now? Probably not entirely. As long as we huff and puff ourselves, we are predisposed to train our children to do likewise. However, human beings are capable of enormous self-control and change in the interests of their children's well-being. I have seen it happen. In fact, I have found that if I can make parents see what they are doing and how it affects the child, they are often able to stop.

I remember Sue's parents, who came to me because their ten-year-old daughter had stopped doing her schoolwork in spite of every form of discipline they could think of. A few days earlier her teacher had told them that Sue and her best friend were often missing after lunch—apparently playing hooky together.

What was the matter? These parents had both grown up in a small Iowa farm town. School, from first grade through the university, was a breeze. Now they were bringing up a child in the most sophisticated, high-pressured urban center in the world. Obviously, they had decided—without even saying it to each other—that what was good enough for them would *never*, NEVER do for Sue. They put her in the most competitive private school, which took some pushing and plenty of financial sacrifice. They checked up on every day's progress in every subject, reminding her often of how important her every move might be. The daily parental checkup, and the tremendous responsibility the child felt, made her so nervous that she had to escape. In the only way a child knows, she was begging to be allowed to live her own life.

Somehow my experience and perhaps my professional authority gave Sue's parents the initial confidence they needed to stop worrying and do as their parents had done with them: i.e. assume that Sue would learn. They began to let her alone. When she realized she was on her own, she returned to being the enthusiastic, conscientious student she had been at the start.

Another couple I saw had a son with a real learning problem. With proper remedial help, he was making very good progress. However, he had a long way to go. It was getting close to the end of the school year, and we had to decide whether to advise the school to promote him. I felt sure he could catch up with his classmates before the end of the year to come, but I wasn't sure that he should have to struggle that hard. He had been under a strain for so long that I had some fear that another year of it might dampen his enthusiasm for learning permanently.

The issue was—should he stay behind and enjoy his work and build up some confidence, or go ahead, on the theory that his pride in finally catching up would carry him through?

I explained all this to his parents. His mother listened thoughtfully. His father vetoed the mere suggestion that Stevie repeat fourth grade. He said the humiliation would finish him.

I tried to explain again how important it was for Steve's academic future to make a decision that would not overburden him just as he was beginning to catch up. I felt he would recover quickly from the decision to repeat the grade, as long as his teacher and parents put it to him positively. I had a hunch that Steve would breathe a sigh of relief if they suggested he stay back. I said so. However, I suggested waiting until after the yearly achievement tests, and getting his teacher's advice then, before making a final decision.

Suddenly the father reversed himself. "You're absolutely right, he should stay back. Let's let him off the hook. I wasn't thinking about him. All I was worrying about was 'how can I tell my brother that a child of mine had to repeat a grade.' I'm not saying I'm not going to be ashamed. But damned if I'm going to hurt Stevie for it." That father kept his word.

Sometimes parents can handle children's school troubles better if I can help them see the immediate problem in perspective. School problems arouse so much anxiety that parents sometimes can't talk of anything except what's wrong with Johnny when I first see them. They begin with a simple fact: teacher says five-year-old Johnny is careless. Then, upset by this really minor adverse comment, go on to tell me that he leaves his mittens in school, always misplaces his pencil, doesn't pick up his toys, and forgets to say "thank you" to his grandmother. This leads to a string of awful predictions: He won't make friends, or impress college admissions directors and employment agencies; and he will inevitably fail at marriage.

Aside from being nonsense, none of this helps solve the immediate problem, or even explain it.

I try to shift the focus from Johnny's faults and Mommy's fears by asking questions that elicit a factual picture of Johnny. This device—try it yourself the next time you have black thoughts about your child's behavior—puts Johnny in a better perspective. He stops being all problem—a monster dripping with error, and becomes, once more, a living, breathing, feeling individual with at least a few possibilities. It is important to try to keep problems from blocking out the child.

It also helps to think about the immediate question in terms of your long-term goals for your family. Parents have trouble doing this. They tend to treat first grade behavior as if it were the ultimate test of a child's ability to cope with life in the adult world. An F in effort or a C in arithmetic is seen as a permanent blemish to parents who know that Berkeley requires an A average in high school. Actually, first grade work does not necessarily foreshadow what will happen in second grade, let alone high school. And academic success, even in college, is not a guarantee of success in the adult world.

It is easier to sort out real problems from ones that could be ignored, if you bear in mind what the goals of elementary education are. If you remember what grade school children are supposed to accomplish, you can judge more soundly just how a first-grader's problem, for example, is going to affect his long-term academic progress.

Here are the broad guidelines I would use.

1. *Mastery.* Children who cannot add, subtract, multiply, and divide, read easily, and write simple paragraphs are so hobbled when they face high school work that they may be tempted to give up learning before they have really sampled what it can mean for them in adult life.

Children should finish sixth grade at the age of eleven or twelve with a solid command of the tool subjects—reading, writing, and arithmetic—by whatever names they are called in their particular schools.

Some children are fairly competent by the end of third grade. Some struggle with writing and arithmetic right through fifth grade. How far along a child is at any given point is not as important as whether he is making steady progress. If he isn't I would want to check up.

2. *Study skills.* The elementary grades should teach children how to go about learning so that they know how to find out what they *don't* know. It is not natural for a child to cry over homework; fight about it with his parents; fall apart when he is asked to do a problem at the blackboard; or simply fail to do it night after night on the grounds that he doesn't know how.

When teacher-parent-child relations are working reasonably well, an elementary school child should be able to tackle his homework by himself. He should have a repertory of things to do when he gets stuck on any assignment.

A. Try again.

B. Review in the book and see if he can't refresh his memory.

C. Call a friend.

D. Ask his parents for help.

E. Wait until class and get help from the teacher.

If a child seems consistently unable to get his work done, parents should find out why.

3. *Enjoyment.* Normally, children are interested in learning. It should be rewarding enough as a whole to make the dull and hard parts worth struggling through.

When you make cookies with a small child he learns an incredible variety of things: number and size concepts; how things work; what they taste like; how to cut out, bake, and eat, and last of all clean up.

Different parts of the job are favorites for different children. Some are in it simply for the finished product. But all children that I know enjoy making cookies enough to put up with the dull part—cleaning up; and the hard part—stirring, cutting, and transferring uncooked cookies, undamaged, to the cookie sheet.

Normally, they feel the same way about school. They like it, even when they do some of the dull part (drill) and the hard part (new lessons) reluctantly.

The first grades should make children feel good about school. If a child is unwilling to go, apathetic, actively rebellious, or simply miserable when he is there, I'd be concerned. If the negative attitude continues for more than a few weeks, I'd investigate. You certainly don't want your children fed up with learning before they get to high school.

In a society that values wide knowledge, professional and technical skills, and performance, it's as natural for children to want to succeed in school as it is for them to want to master the games, sports, and hobbies of their elders. To understand how you can encourage them and help them, it is important to understand how children learn.

2

WHAT HELPS CHILDREN LEARN

The Parents' Role

Babies learn more in the first two years than they do all the rest of their lives. They work so hard and so constantly, and learn so steadily and fast that parents not only don't worry about how things are going, they don't even stop to think what a stupendous feat the child's first two years of learning are.

Your child's development seems to happen, just the way physical growth does. But, although children are born with a built-in capacity and will to learn, they would never make it to first grade without your help.

It may all start with the first smile. Your baby is totally dependent on outside help for survival. Lying alone in his cool bassinet, hunger must be his dominant sensation. The food deliveries somehow keep coming. His hunger cries gradually become less anguished. He makes out the smile of the food deliverer. He manages a feeble smile in return. Somewhere in those first months he gets the idea that smiling is rewarded. He pleases for his food at first. But fond grown-ups do so much to make him happy as he continues to grow—cuddling, candy, singing, comforting, playing ball, bringing toys —that he ends up trying to please them, spontaneously.

Children learn because the grown-ups they care about want them to. You are their models. They learn because they want to be like you.

You don't realize you are teaching because you fall into it as naturally as your child falls into learning. When a child tries to please you, you coo, praise, clap, and caress. In these ways you constantly reinforce and encourage children's eagerness to learn. You also stimulate their curiosity.

You talk to your baby, tell stories, and introduce him to the world around him long before he can talk back.

Hear yourself teaching your first-born during his first two years, when you are totally unaware of what you are doing:

Parent (to Johnny—4 months—in carriage) Look, Johnny, there's a dog. See him? Woof, woof!

Johnny smiles, giggles, wriggles.

Parent (to Johnny in high chair, 6 months) Hear that, Johnny? Bow, wow! What's that? That's the dog barking outside.

Johnny (more giggles and wriggles)

Parent (to Johnny in stroller, 12 months) Here comes the dog, Johnny. Want to pat him? (You take his hand and rub it over the dog's soft fur.) Nice soft doggy.

Johnny Mmm. (Laughing and looking at you)

Johnny (riding in car—16 months, jumping up and down in his seat) Dog, dog. Woof! Woof!

Father Hey, look at you. You talked. You said "dog."

Mother That's right, Johnny. That's a nice soft dog. Woof, woof! Bow, wow! Look, Johnny, there's a horse over there near the red barn. Say "horse."

Parents help children learn by letting them alone, too.

You seem to know instinctively just how much to encourage. You don't overdo it. You also know how much to help and how much to protect. You don't hover over your child and talk so much that he never has a chance to try new things on his own. As a result, your child gets plenty of chance to explore and master things all by himself. When he succeeds he has an enormous sense of achievement.

"I did it. I did it," you'll hear a little child say with total joy. "I tied my shoes myself, Mommy."

I have fun watching parents when they don't know anyone is looking. The other day I watched a lovely little parent-child vignette unfold from the window where I was doing some writing.

A young mother was walking slowly down the street pushing a stroller full of groceries. She got to the steps of her apartment building; pulled the stroller up; opened the door and pushed it in. Then she stood on the steps watching.

I followed her glance. Down the sidewalk came her two-year-old, strutting along as if he owned the city. A few months ago I had seen him bundled into that stroller; strapped and wrapped tight in blankets; pushed by this grown-up; lifted out by her; held onto wherever he went. Now he's on his own. He examines the cracks in the sidewalk; stops on the steps he passes. He won't go into the street. His mother trusts him.

He gets to the steps. Each one is as high as his legs are long. He has a cracker box in his hand. He tries to lift his leg to mount the step. He can't make it. The grown-up watches and waits. He looks at her for help. She smiles and waits. He tries again. No luck. He looks at the box. He looks at the railing. He looks at the grown-up again. She smiles. He takes hold of the railing and tries. No good. Still holding the railing he stops to think. He looks at the box. He puts it down on the step. Now he leans on the steps with his free hands and balances himself so he can make the step. He's up. He looks at his mother, smiling now himself. She smiles again. He picks up the box, recognizes he's got the same problem again. But this time he doesn't give up the box. He gets up the next step leaning on the box in his hand. Next step he tries without using the box hand at all. Can't make it. Legs are too short. He leans on the box again. He's up. He's made all the steps. His mother hugs him to her, impulsively, and carries him through the door.

You know how to suit lessons to the age and stage of your child.

You don't expect too much. You don't ask too little. You make learning attractive. A two-year-old like the fellow I watched getting up the steps the other day, is just beginning to play with cars and blocks. If I know two-year-olds, his room is probably a shambles by suppertime. Of course, he's much too little to understand about being neat and tidy, but is he too young to begin to understand?

His father comes in to get him for supper—let's imagine. He says, "Time to clean up. Supper's ready." That's all. Then he starts putting the boy's cars together in a line.

He says, "Look what I'm doing. Isn't this a good garage? What car shall I put in next?"

The little boy is hooked. He runs around filling his arms with cars and bringing them to his daddy. "Dis ones, dis ones. Here dis bus one." He is helping. He is beginning to get the idea of picking up, although he may not be expected to clean up alone until he is five or so.

He starts learning with lessons scaled to his capacity to take them in, taught in snatches that are brief enough to hold his still short span of attention.

Each new lesson is based on what has gone before.

When the two becomes a three, he'll pick up some by himself, when his father, getting supper, calls, "Let's start cleaning up." Before he gets tired, though, his father will come and help. At five or six, depending on his style and rate of development, and family expectations, he'll be able to do the whole clean-up job; sometimes without even being reminded. He'll also have the book he wants to hear picked out (if that's the bedtime routine in his house). Then, if a grown-up stops in the middle of a sentence of a familiar story, he'll finish it himself, from memory.

Parents are patient when children practice.

You have probably reached the point as I have, when you would like to explode over a three-year-old's endless *WHYS*. In fact, I suppose you have exploded: "I've told you that a million times. No more whys. I just told you." Every parent does. At the same time every parent answers about a hundred whys for every once he is impatient. And once in about every 150 whys you see that the endless answering was worth it.

Children may say why to get attention. They may say why because they are tired and bored and have nothing else to do. But most of the time WHY? is a kind of Little Leaguer's practice session for toddlers. The Little Leaguer practices over and over again, throwing a curve, with a persistence that is phenomenal. It is this same kind of persistence that makes a toddler ask why again and again, about something his father and mother have told him again and again.

Each time you answer he listens, busily trying to put it together as you talk. Each time you answer he fits in a few more of the pieces, until finally, he has learned something new.

I'll give you one of my favorite examples. My friend's granddaughter came with her for a visit last year and I took her to a dairy farm near my country retreat. She was two, but very talkative.

I expected she'd like the calves and the tractors, but we arrived just as one of the dairymen was cleaning the pasteurizing room. He was hosing down the floor and sweeping the water to the drain. Sara looked at the new calves, the machines, sat on one big tractor, dutifully. But she was doing it only to please me. The only thing she really cared about was the man sweeping.

All during the rest of our tour and all the way home she asked, "Whaffor da man sweep da floor?"

As soon as I answered, she asked again. If I told her once, I told her twenty-five times. I was so fascinated by her persistence that I answered in much too grand detail, giving her all the reasons for sanitation in dairy barns.

When I got tired I tried to change the subject to the horses and flowers in the fields, or the bright-colored cars on the road. No luck. Finally we were home and her grandmother came out to greet us.

"What did you see, Sara?" she asked.

"Da man was sweeping da floor," she began—and proceeded almost without help to give a pretty reasonable account of what he was doing and why it was necessary.

It was a vivid illustration of how the wheels in the little child's head go around. It's hard for someone who has been around—even as long as a young parent has—to remember what a lot there is for a little child to learn in order even to begin to understand her immediate world. Children learn in these practice sessions. Sometimes they are question periods in which children quiz the adults around them who know what it's all about. Sometimes they are trial and error periods—through which they test the environment.

Most parents show incredible patience with children's practice sessions. They don't just grin and bear the endless questions, and the "stupid" mistakes. They often show almost as much enthusiasm in answering as children do for finding out.

Good teachers want children to ask questions because the questions tell them what they need to teach. *They encourage questions, because they want to keep children's curiosity alive. They are also sympathetic to children's sometimes ill-fated attempts to do things on their own, because they want to keep their initiative and independence thriving.* Children who are afraid to ask questions and afraid to experiment soon stop learning.

Parents don't have to worry about being good teachers. They teach instinctively, and have enormous patience and interest in helping little children get up in the world.

3

PRESCHOOL SCHOOLING

How Much Should You Try to Teach

Children used to start school when they got there—in first grade, at five, or six. They had already mastered innumerable skills and acquired an encyclopedic amount of information. But nobody set out, systematically, to teach them.

Children learned words, number concepts, rhythm, rhyme, and plain facts from games like pat-a-cake, peek-a-boo, ride-away-to-Boston; from skip-rope and ball-bouncing jingles; from Mother Goose and folk songs. They knew something about how babies are born and African geography from visits to the zoo with their parents. They learned about cars, machines, cows, horses, barns, tractors, crops, and seasons from their toys and from leisurely chatter on car trips. They put the bus fare in the fare box and began to understand about money. They counted bananas or picked out the right soap powder for the shopping cart and began to understand counting and the equivalent of reading readiness. Play with pots and pans, empty cartons, spools, bottle tops and lids, taught them about sizes and shapes.

In olden times—as one of our children used to call the age before her birth—a parent answering a child's questions, or showing him how to fit the pans together on the closet shelf, wasn't purposely instructing him. If you asked the parent what he was doing, he'd say: "Playing." "Entertaining. Long drives are hard for kids." "Explaining." "Amusing myself watching Timmy's head work."

Now it's different. Some parents start thinking about their children's formal education before they are born. Every neighborhood stationery store has shelves packed tight with educational toys for use in a curriculum that begins as soon—postpartum—as mother is up to holding classes.

Bus cards and newspaper and magazine ads appeal to conscientious, "good" parents to buy this, subscribe to that, enroll the toddler in any one of a number of academic, psychological, or scientific play groups to raise his IQ. Ph.D.'s—real and phony—set up academies to groom the preschooler for admission to the nursery school of his parents' choice. Reading, early math, and middle class morality are propagated by puppets on the home screen, to moppets with workbooks and pencils at the ready. Nursery school today is looked on as serious academic business; a leg up on the ladder to that springboard to adult success—the right college.

Last month, for example, an obviously devoted father and mother came to me with their three-year-old because the nursery school teacher had told them her attention span was too short for her age. I couldn't help smiling, and in an effort to allay their fears about their perfectly normal lively little girl I said, "You must be worried about college?"

Without a flicker of a smile, they answered, "Yes." It was clearly no joking matter.

The toddler's academic performance can stir up as much anxiety these days as the college-bound junior's SAT scores did at the peak of the college boom five years ago. The steady decline in reading levels in city schools and the emergence of the dropout—first from college and now from high school—as a permanent part of the national scene are partly responsible. So, too, are the daily, sometimes hourly bulletins via TV, press, and periodical—on the untapped mental capabilities of the very young and the family's baleful influence on child development. Parents are bound to feel, from what they read and hear, that their children's success in school depends almost entirely on them. Naturally they dig in and start teaching, worrying more or less constantly about whether they are using the right methods, the right equipment, and—even harder to evaluate—the right approach.

Sometimes, it seems to me that we would be better off if the explosion in knowledge about the "learnability" of the young had never happened. This may sound strange from someone who has devoted a great part of a professional career to research in child development. Of course, I am not seriously in favor of turning the clock back on scientific progress. But I am horrified at how we have distorted and exploited what we have learned about children for the wrong purposes.

Sometimes investigators themselves are to blame. Overenthusiastic about their work, they burst into headlines, prematurely, with findings that radically change previous theories. Then they contradict themselves, or are contradicted later by equally compelling, new evidence. Before the ink is dry on scholarly reports, journalists, teachers, pediatricians, and others seize the news, and put it to work to sell books, magazines, papers, toys, or what have you.

Young, conscientious parents, brought up to believe that the newest is the best, are the most likely victims. They distrust whatever their parents did; have little experience to temper their judgment, and embrace the latest, most loudly touted pronouncements on child rearing as gospel.

Read properly, what we have found out about learning and development in this century indicates that children with average health and mentality will get along just fine in school if they have average homes and normally interested and affectionate parents. Parents, however, get the scary news that emotional environment and proper stimulation are crucial; and that failure to provide both, in carefully prescribed quantities, at the right time, may lead to permanent damage. One aspect or another of a study is taken out of context, blown up out of all proportion, to produce a composite picture of the hazards of child rearing.

In the interest of making childhood easier and more fun for parents, as well as for children, I would like to correct some of the distortions.

Most of what we have found out in this century comes from the famous Swiss child psychologist Jean Piaget's studies of how children learn and develop understanding; and from Americans who have concentrated on the effect of environment on the development of motivation and cognitive ability.

To summarize Piaget, very simply: He found that children, at a given age level, all see the world in the same general way. Their perceptions and conceptions of what goes on around them mature according to a standard timetable. However, within this framework, the rate of development, and the areas in which a child becomes sophisticated, vary according to individual interest, capacity, and style, and the kinds and quality of stimulation from the environment.

It's easy to see how practical-minded educators could infer from this, that pump-priming nursery-age children with formal lessons would speed up learning in first grade and accelerate the conventional educational program. But this reasoning ignores Piaget's basic tenet—the standard timetable. There is just so much a child can take in—no matter how many forms of stimulus he gets.

Piaget has been talking to, playing with, and watching children of all ages—from infancy to adolescence for forty years. He discovered the pattern of their mental development by comparing their evolving understanding of a great many things they all think about, from the way of the wind, the flow of water, the working of bicycles and machines, to right and wrong.

His own children were the guinea pigs for some of his original observations. A game he played with babies —a form of peek-a-boo—shows how unyielding the course of development is right from the beginning. He put a puppet in one hand; held a scarf in the other; displayed both to the baby. Then he covered the puppet with the scarf and showed that. Next he removed the scarf and revealed the puppet again. Question: When would a baby get the point and start looking for the puppet to show up under the scarf?

At four months the baby shows no interest in the game at all, no matter how many times it is played. Somewhere between a year and eighteen months, even a baby who has never played the game before notices where the puppet has disappeared and keeps his eye on the scarf until the puppet is exposed again.

Babies don't take this big leap forward until a number of things, clearly beyond the control of human manipulation, have taken place. First, physiological development has to advance. The time this takes is more or less standard and fixed. Second, they have to get experience —sensory understanding of the appearing-disappearing phenomenon. Finally, there has to be a consolidation, a kind of $1 + 1 = 2$. The baby sees better, hears better, has had learning practice, from many observations of appearing, disappearing, and reappearing objects. All these factors finally combine to make him able to anticipate a certain outcome from a sequence of events.

To generalize from this example, the gradual maturing of understanding depends on the *many* factors involved in development working *together:* 1. Biological age. 2. Environment (what there is to learn). 3. Stimulation and practice (what people do with him).

Without stimulation and practice children would not advance at all. But no matter how much stimulation they get in crib, playpen, or toddler days, and how much encouragement they have to push, pull, fit, try, wonder, look, compare, question, listen, etc., there is just so much they are capable of grasping at a given age. Their minds cannot outstrip the age-determined level of their perceptual and conceptual development. This, in turn, depends on the motory and sensory experience they have had, which takes a specific period of time to accumulate.

When I was four, I was trying hard, like most younger children, to catch up to my big sister, already in school. I wanted to be able to read. But the best I could do was get read to. My superior sister used me to practice her new lessons and review her old ones. Every day after school, she read to me from her primer until I knew it by heart.

Our sixty-year-old grandmother, who lived with us, saw all this and decided she wanted to learn to read English. I proudly volunteered to teach her and sat down beside her, moving my finger from word to word in my sister's book, as I had watched her do, and "reading," "Run, run, Henny Penny . . ."

I taught my grandmother to read. It made me a genius in her eyes. My mother told her I was simply parroting what I knew by heart. She remained unconvinced. Ironically, in first grade, it turned out that I was dyslexic (Chapter 14). I did not really read until I had had a summer's corrective drill.

At four I had mastered the superficial aspects of reading—the sounds, the motions, the connection between print and sound. But, despite all the practice my sister gave me, I was incapable of putting it together to mean anything to me.

Recently, in a game of darts with a nine-year-old, I scored a bull's-eye. While I was writing down my ten, he moved my dart to the three circle. Then he looked at the score card and said, "That's wrong. You got a three. Look!"

If he had been three or even five I would have let it pass, knowing he was too young to understand rules. But he was nine, so I said, with a smile, "I know it's on the three circle now. But you can't fool me. I saw where you moved it from." He laughed with me and put my dart back in the bull's-eye.

You will develop a sort of sixth sense about what your children are ready for. It will tell you, better than books, or the blurbs on educational toys, what, how much, and when to teach.

When Piaget was in this country in 1972 a student asked him how his work could be used to accelerate the education of the young. Piaget scoffed, "That's an American dilemma."

Americans, however, are not all obsessed with speeding up their children's intellectual development. Many parents are simply anxious that their failure to provide the right stimulation at the right time might stunt their children's intellectual growth. They have been influenced by the widely quoted studies of the thirties and forties that showed that children who are deprived in their early years are permanently crippled, mentally, physically, and emotionally.

You don't need to worry.

Those children had not only been separated from their parents prematurely, they were raised in institutions where no attempt was made to provide proper parent substitutes. The only stimulation they got was from a shifting cast of caretakers who gave them little more than routine physical care. The average parent could not duplicate such conditions if he tried. As a matter of fact, even if he succeeded the effects would not necessarily be permanent, according to the latest evidence.

Two years ago a British medical journal published a report from Czechoslovakia about the gradual rehabilitation of twins who had been systematically brutalized from the age of one and a half to six by a Grimms' fairy-tale-type stepmother. She kept them in a cellar room, isolated from their four siblings. At first she merely fed them and ignored them. Later she mistreated them brutally and encouraged the other children to join in the abuse. The neighbors heard animal howls coming from the cellar, but kept their distance, unwilling to tangle with this formidable woman. A relative of the children's natural mother reported the stepmother to the authorities. Nothing happened. The situation was finally uncovered when the father took one of the boys to a pediatrician to have him certified as unfit for primary school. The child, then six, looked three, could barely walk, was afraid of noise, movements, traffic, people. He seemed severely retarded. The pediatrician initiated an investigation that led to the removal and rehabilitation of the boys and the trial of the parents for criminal neglect.

The most fantastic part of the story is the conclusion. After five years of institutional and foster home care and intensive therapy the children were functioning almost at their age level (eleven) mentally, emotionally, and physically, and were still improving.

I cannot believe that many children would recover from the experience they had. Perhaps their twinship—the company they gave each other—saved them. Nevertheless the story does illustrate the remarkable tenacity of children's will to survive and their amazing durability.

Even more persuasive evidence of this comes from a report by Jerome Kagan, a Harvard child psychologist, on childhood in a Guatemalan Indian village. Babies there spend their first eighteen months indoors in dark, smoke-filled huts. Their mothers are affectionate and spend long periods cradling and nursing them. However, no one talks to them or plays with them. They don't even see daylight.

At a year and a half they act like nine-month-old babies, severely retarded by our standards. However, at five, they are lively, bright, and thoroughly normal, also by our standards. Almost total lack of visual and verbal stimulation during a period of fantastic development for American children doesn't seem to alter their final development at all.

Children grow up mentally, as they do physically, almost inevitably. The specific things they learn and the timetable for learning them will vary from culture to culture. The Guatemalan Indian in a remote village is not going to have any understanding of the dynamics of a jet engine when he's sixteen, the way a middle class American boy does. Babies are programmed to learn to cope with the environment into which they are born, and human parents are programmed, by their culture, to bring them up. You can't help stimulating and directly teaching your babies unless you're an ogre.

You don't have to coach them for first grade. The schools' curriculum from grade to grade is geared to the average child's ability to take the lessons in. Children can usually coast into first grade just the way you did before them, on the wisdom they absorb in their first five years at home and in nursery school and kindergarten.

I know I will not dissuade you from trying the latest educational equipment, toys, games, puzzles, with your preschooler. I would not want to. Even if children do not need to be systemically taught, parents can't resist the urge to play with them, challenge and test them. Watching a human being become aware and begin to show signs of responding and understanding is part of the fun of parenthood. Most children enjoy this kind of fun, too. They love to try to be just a little bit bigger and more like their older brothers and sisters, the kid next door, or their mothers and fathers. As long as you realize that your formal teaching is not going to change the long-range academic progress of your toddler very much; and don't take yourself or your child too seriously, you won't do any damage.

There is no sure-fire formula; no one, two, three set of do's and don't's. It is safe to say, however, that what is fun for you is generally fun for your child. I have seen a very high-powered father play games and try riddles on a very smart four-year-old, with lots of roughhousing and tossing in the air between queries and answers, where parent and child were both having a great time.

I have seen the same basic situation in another family that was sheer agony to watch.

What was fun and games for the first father was very serious business for the second. The first father was playful, affectionate, having a good time. His little girl, taking her cue from him, enjoyed it, too. There were no penalties—except a hug, or a toss in the air—when she didn't come through with the right answer. She was temperamentally so bouncy, that even criticism would probably not have dampened her spirits. When she lost interest he ended the game.

The second father cared desperately about whether his four-year-old would learn to catch the ball, *now*. The child was very sensitive, and felt the tension, and wilted even as he tried to please. It wasn't a game. It was a contest. Father wasn't fun. He was a coach with a scoreboard, constantly checking performance; anxious about whether his son would measure up. Finally the child fell down, crying more than he needed to. It was the game, not the bruise that hurt him. And he had to end it.

You don't have to be a child development expert to know when your lessons are over your pupil's head. You may be fooled, like my grandmother was, by a momentary show of sophistication in a small child. But when you start teaching you'll quickly find out the difference between the accidental flash of brilliance and true wisdom. My daughter-in-law took our three-year-old grandchild to buy a dress. The salesperson brought out a supply, but none of them suited. Suddenly Laurie noticed a red dress on a hanger and piped up, "I want that red dress." The salesperson was bowled over.

"That baby knows her colors already?" she said admiringly.

Laurie's mother accepted the compliment gracefully, but she knew that Laurie couldn't really tell her colors. Red is the first color babies notice; therefore the first color they recognize, and finally name. Laurie did know red, but it was the only color she could name. Her mother might drill her daily, by naming each object she referred to with its color, but, although Laurie can match colors, now, indicating that she can tell them apart, she will not be able to give them their right names, consistently, until she is about five, probably, and has had lots of practice making mistakes.

Learning through the natural give and take of parent-child relations is the best way for children. If a child asks you the color of something, tell him. Of course you won't be able to resist asking him the color of something else. But, if he doesn't want to tell you, don't press. If he gives the wrong answer, don't make a big point of correcting him. Tell him the right color or say something harmless like "That's nice." Then move on to another subject. There will be plenty of other opportunities for him to get practice on colors. Wait until he asks the name of a color again. You will probably find that he has already made progress in telling them apart and naming them correctly.

There is undoubtedly a book that lets you know just

when children know just what. Forget the book. Children vary enormously. Common sense will tell you whether your child is progressing satisfactorily. Don't get hung up on whether he's learning at top, intermediate, or slow speed.

Like many other aspects of behavior, the way a child learns comes down to temperament. There are quick learners who may not get all the details of the assignment or the lesson; slow learners who seem to work things out inside, silently and persistently, before they show any signs of learning anything at all; and children who ask questions, without waiting for answers—asking the same thing over and over, long before they *really hear* your reply.

Although I have recommended going very lightly on any formal preschool teaching, I would make an exception with children whose temperamental qualities might handicap them when they get to school. Be careful not to become embattled with the child in your efforts to minimize his problems but don't ignore them. For example, if you have a son or daughter who asks the same question over and over, then dashes off before you have time to answer, you can find ways to surprise him into listening. You can make him aware of his tendency to be easily distracted. You don't have to punish him or make him uncomfortable to do it. You may even be able to kid him into paying attention, or train him with treats for showing he has listened.

You might, for example, say to your five-year-old on a Saturday morning at breakfast, "I've been thinking about what we could do today. I thought up a game. I'm going to ask you three questions, one at a time. If you can answer two of them right we'll go out and I'll help you practice on your bike to see if you can't get rid of those old training wheels."

The point, of course, is to give him an incentive for learning to pay attention. Make the questions easy, so you're sure he can answer two without any trouble. They might be 1. What color is that shirt you have on? 2. Which is the biggest cup on the breakfast table? 3. What did you have for dessert last night?

This game can go on being fun for some time. When it has achieved its purpose you can take it a step further. Surprise him the next time he asks a question, by saying, "If you can repeat the answer I give you right back to me, I'm going to give you a special treat."

The treats don't need to be enormous—a story he likes, a card trick he enjoys watching, or a chance to go for an ice cream cone. This kind of positive re-enforcement of what you want to teach works infinitely better than scolding, and plain, dull drill.

Are you worried about overstimulating your children? Making them too high-strung? During one of the many pendulum swings in child care practice in this century, parents were warned against just this. Too much stimulation was supposed to lead to nervous exhaustion and mental breakdown in children. That myth has been laid to rest like many other fads and phobias in child care. Children tell you when they have had too much. If you are sensitive to your child's reactions, and cease and desist from formal teaching efforts when a child shows confusion, fatigue, bad temper, or inability to grasp what you are trying to get across, he won't suffer.

Many people were appalled a few years ago when parents—on someone's advice—started putting big labels on everything in the house so babies would get reading readiness with their bottles. It may have been ridiculous, but it was harmless.

Bats, in their blindness, have an internal radar system to warn them when they are approaching objects, so they don't fly into things, head on. Babies have some kind of radar system, too. It screens out the sounds, sights, ideas that they are not ready to absorb and picks up what they can make sense of at the moment.

I can't think of any good scientific reason to justify my own personal aversion to seeing playpens and nursery shelves so crowded with toys and bits and pieces of toys that there's hardly space left to play in. But the fact is that the children who have the most often play the least. Maybe too many toys are a sign of too little *human* stimulation. No matter how superior the educational value of the toys parents buy, they never take the place of what parents or other grown-ups contribute to play. Children need toys. They should have times to play alone. But, in the very early years, loving, interested grown-ups offer a kind of stimulation that nothing else does. Their presence automatically adds a dimension: someone to show you something; someone to show something to; someone to react, watch, smile, applaud—a reason to expand, elaborate, and experiment.

I have said, repeatedly, that children, almost in spite of you, will learn what they need to know for first grade. That is not true for all of our children—particularly those who don't speak standard English, or any English at all, and others who, for a variety of economic or social reasons, have not been baptized in the prevailing culture of the middle class.

In the best of all possible worlds, teachers would find out what each first-grader knew when he got to school, and begin teaching him there. In the here and now, however, teachers usually begin teaching at the mythical standard level where all first-graders are supposed to be. They label those who aren't there stupid, instead of helping them catch up on what they need to know.

Lack of preparation for the standard first grade curriculum can then doom these children to failure for life. Schools have been excusing themselves by leaning on the theory that lack of proper stimulation in early childhood has caused irreparable mental retardation, making the untaught unteachable. We know this is nonsense. Physically and mentally healthy children learn what their environment expects if they get the message. Puerto Rican-born parents don't expect the same things of their children that American middle class parents do. Therefore, when the children reach first grade they often have not learned what the average middle class teacher expects them to know.

Parents should insist that schools and teachers change their expectations, and teach all first-graders what they need to know. Until they do, minority group parents would be wise to prepare their children systematically, if they are to get a good start.

What should you teach? You might visit your neighborhood school for advice. If that's not convenient, here is a basic list to start with: How to tell shapes, including squares, circles, triangles; how to tell colors; directions, such as up, down, left, right, behind, in front of; comparisons, such as big, bigger, biggest; how to read and write your name; how to follow instructions and carry out simple little jobs around the house.

What kinds of instructions? Brush your teeth. Turn off the water. Button your coat. Bring out your plate. Bring me your book. Empty all the wastebaskets. Make the baby laugh, and so on.

What games and toys will help? You don't need to buy elaborate toys and equipment. Children can learn shapes and sizes from your kitchen pots and pans and magazine pictures. They can learn to concentrate from simple card games every parent can play, or from playing a game with you where they look at several simple objects you have put on the table, then tell you which one you have removed, while they had their eyes closed. In general, the more you talk to them, the more you show them, the more you read with them, talking about the story and asking them questions about it as you go along, and the more fun you have together, the better prepared they will be to learn from their first grade teacher.

4

HOW TO HELP THE TEACHER HELP YOUR CHILD

Children are naturally interested in going to school. If they have started to learn eagerly and easily at home, they usually go right on that way. Their first real books are as interesting to them as new toys are. They can't wait to get homework like their big brothers and sisters. They think workbooks are as much fun as "free play."

Even ordinary parents are extraordinary teachers during a child's early years.

Without realizing what they are doing, they stimulate, guide, encourage curiosity and independence, suit demands to children's special needs and abilities, help when asked, encourage increasing responsibility and independence, and much more.

Sometimes, though, they forget what good teachers they are when children start school. Suddenly the child is learning with a capital L. Learning is very important. Parents become intimidated by teachers, lose confidence in their judgment about the child, and assume that teacher knows best.

Not so!

Remember the skills you possess and exercise so

naturally. Use them to help your child with schoolwork, to keep track of what is happening in school, and to evaluate his progress. If you do, you can be sure that he will get along better and enjoy learning more.

Try, too, to remember your child, all through his school life, as the eager learner he was at home. It will help you duplicate the environment for learning that nourished him so well at the beginning.

Don't anticipate problems. They are rare, and not usually serious to start with. Keeping the basic premises of a good learning situation in mind will help you avoid them altogether.

1. *Children need success.* It encourages new effort. Pleasure in achievement is very human. An eight-month-old baby will look triumphant, almost ecstatic, when he has wriggled seal-like across the floor and finally clutched the bright red ball. Who knows why? But who denies it?

Sometimes children lose interest in school because they don't feel they are getting anywhere. This may be because someone—you or the teacher—has made them feel that they are not doing what is expected. If you think this is a possibility, get together with your child's teacher and decide what you feel is reasonable to expect at this moment. Perhaps you will both lower your sights, temporarily, in the interest of raising your child's will and enthusiasm for learning.

You may find that, by objective standards, your child is not up to working at the speed and level that is demanded. In that case, you and his teacher will have to consider whether to transfer him to a less demanding class, or school, or arrange to give him the kind of help he needs to catch up.

Another thing. Every child has some particular skill or talent he likes to exercise, whether it is shoveling snow, weeding the garden, playing the harmonica, or taking care of the baby next door. A good time to recognize his special abilities is when he is having blue Mondays because of lack of success at school. Letting him know how good he is won't erase the school problem, but it will certainly buck up his courage to work on it.

Supposing you or the teacher decides that one of you is setting impossible standards. If the teacher is guilty there isn't much you can do about it, except wait until next year, and try—in the meantime—to make your child feel that you believe he is doing very well. However, if you decide that you are the one who is asking too much, try to lower your sights. Unrealistic demands set the stage for your child's failure. When you ask what is truly impossible, the strain of perpetually trying and failing is bound to discourage a child from trying at all.

2. *Children need applause.* It's human to want love and approval: a smile, an approving pat, words of praise.

Learning requires repetitive trials and errors. That takes a lot of persistence and courage. Many times children give up because effort is not respected, let alone rewarded. Adults often make fun of children's mistakes and "foolish" questions, and forget to praise the effort and interest they have shown. Scolding, scoffing, and teasing make children fearful.

3. *Lessons have to begin where the child is.* Many, many children get off to a bad start in school simply because their teachers insist on teaching a curriculum instead of children. When a child has not had the foundation that the curriculum is based on, he is out of luck.

A thoughtless teacher can often turn a child off by treating his inexperience as laziness, inattention, or stupidity. Instead of quietly seeing how much each child in first grade knows at the start: how to say the A B C's, to write his name, to recognize certain words and sounds, and then teaching them what they don't know, she begins comparing: "Luis can't even write his name yet"; or "Isn't Mary smart? She knows all her letters."

If you find your child is unhappy because he does not know what his teacher wants him to, find out where the gaps are. Enlist the teacher's help in filling them.

Some schools have special teachers to give special work to the children who need it. Some schools section children in the first grades so that learning can begin where each child is. But, if the school cannot give your child a good start, perhaps you can help yourself. Simply by seeing the teacher, and offering to help, you will make her more attentive to your child's progress. By suggesting that he is unhappy, you may encourage her to be more helpful and sympathetic to him.

4. *Suit the lesson to the child.* Parents know better than to give little babies their first solid food in adult-sized bites. They cut it up in tiny pieces that go down with little chewing. Nursery school teachers schedule their toddlers' days to fit their capacities: from play period (active and relaxed), to story time (quiet and fairly still), to rhythms (active and organized), to drawing (restful but demanding for small children's still developing muscle control), to refreshment (energy restoring), to rest. Teachers learn from experience that prolonging story time beyond a four-year-old's ability to pay attention doesn't work. When school becomes uncomfortable and difficult for children, learning stops being lovely fun and becomes an awful strain and bore.

In the early grades, particularly, lessons should be planned to suit the children's ability to pay attention.

Any kind of teaching that lasts longer than children can comfortably pay attention fails. If your child is suffering from too rigid a school program, pray that the experience will strengthen his self-control; and hope that next year's teacher will have more enthusiasm for teaching, and less for law and order.

5. *Children are all different.* There is no such thing as the average child, although some are more average than others. Parents instinctively tailor lessons to suit the child. A mother can size up each baby she has in the first few months of his life. Then she begins to accommodate to his particular style. Good teachers do the same thing. Some children learn better by doing. Some learn better by seeing. Some learn better by hearing. Some are faster, some more patient, more restless, distractible, more hesitant, more pushy, and so on.

Occasionally a child will act so differently from the rest that it interferes with other children's learning as well as with his own progress. A teacher may be very ingenious and still be unable to bring such a child into the class program. Ignoring him is hopeless. Clamping down seems to make matters worse—creating bedlam or total withdrawal. However, I have found that parents and teachers working together are sometimes able to help children with difficult temperamental qualities settle down and find some enjoyment and success in school.

Joe, the son of one of the doctors who work with me at the hospital, could not sit still or pay attention for long. This became a problem only when he was in school. His teacher wanted to get him to sit still long enough to listen to directions; and, of course, she had to keep him from disrupting the class. She couldn't waive the rules for him, but she knew he could not realistically be expected to obey them. She found ways for him to move around as often as possible. She called on him to water the plants, to see whether the music room was free, take notes to other teachers—and so on. She broke up his work periods so that he could do the work better. He liked being chosen to help. He is now beginning to enjoy getting praise for doing his work. As a result he is trying harder to sit still and pay attention. To help him, while she is teaching, she calls on him often and brings him back with questions, when she sees him drifting off.

As it happens there is a little girl in the class who is almost Joe's opposite. She is slow, quiet, almost indifferent. In order to get her to get up and move around and do things with the other children, the teacher asks her to do errands with Joe. Joe's teacher was right in guessing that some of his dynamic enthusiasm would rub off on her. They are becoming good friends. They temper each other's natures a little, the way quiet wives and electric husbands sometimes do.

If a child does show disaffection with school in the early grades, don't take it too seriously. The problem may be short-lived. Wait a week or two, to see whether it passes. If it doesn't, review what's happening at home and at school. Most schools are open to parents. Make an appointment and talk things over with the teacher. When you have compared notes, perhaps you can work out a program together that will help make the child happier. Nine times out of ten the problem disappears before your program has had time to take effect. However, on occasion, your efforts fail to produce a happy learner. If a child doesn't make much progress with learning; doesn't seem interested; doesn't want to go to school; is teary and cross when he comes home; and generally unpleasant with friends and relatives, take notice. Don't dally. School problems that persist—whether they center on learning, or on behavior—do not go away by themselves.

The longer a child can't read, the harder it gets for him to catch up. Falling behind is embarrassing. It saps confidence. It destroys the motivation for learning.

Behavior problems isolate children from both teachers and peers. They destroy the motivation for learning, too.

It is best to solve problems before they become too complicated.

Talking to the teacher, that should be your first step. See for yourself what's happening. If the classroom is peaceful, and the children are busy and interested in what they are doing, dismiss the school as a source of trouble and look elsewhere.

If the classroom is hectic and the teacher seems intent on producing a batch of whiz kids, look carefully. You'll recognize the scene. The smart are praised. The slow talkers are referred to the hand wavers for better answers. Several children have their hands in the air and are screaming "I know, I know" all the time any child is trying to talk.

In this kind of atmosphere you can be sure your child, along with many others, is feeling the pressure.

What can you do about it? Talk to other parents. See what they think. If they agree that the teacher pushes too hard, maybe, together, you can persuade teachers and principal to shift from encouraging the children to outperform each other, to involving them all in the business of learning.

This kind of change, when you can effect it, takes time. What can you do to help your child now?

Avoid the temptation to criticize the school. When you do that you excuse your child from trying to cope, to get along with schoolmates and teacher and learn, in spite of the problems.

Instead, try to counteract the dampening effect of school by making a positive climate for learning in the family. That means encouraging conversation. The more you talk, the more easily your child will talk to you. If he talks easily, he will ask questions, and then you will find out what he needs to know and be able to help him.

Answering questions simply and directly encourages children to want to learn. Don't, for example, say, "Haven't you had that in school?" or "Your sister knew that when she was three." Let your child enjoy himself. Don't make conversation, questions, activities into test situations. If a child does something you think is baby-ish, don't say so. For example, don't say, "That's silly. You can draw better flowers than that." Instead say, "That looks like fun." Something encouraging—instead of critical.

Notice when a child does something grown-up, responsible, superior, clever, kind, thoughtful. Notice when he's happy and try to create the kind of situation that he thrives on more often.

Don't push help but give it easily.

If your child's teacher tells you that he has a potentially serious problem, you are bound to be very upset at once. Try not to panic. Listen carefully to what she says. If she asks you to help at home, you will need to follow directions fairly explicitly. If she suggests you consult a specialist, that person will want to know exactly what the teacher has said about school behavior.

It's perfectly natural for parents to be anxious about school problems, but try not to be. Whether a six-year-old gets A's or C's is not half as important as whether he develops interests, makes good friends, learns some responsibility for his own behavior and work, and sustains enjoyment in learning. If you keep your perspective, you can prevent a minor (in the long run) problem from dominating a child's formative years and perhaps clouding his personality for life. In elementary school, children need only the basic skills that high school work demands. Learning problems, if tackled early, can usually be solved before they interfere with that goal.

Sometimes you can help by carefully and coolly following a teacher's instructions. Usually, however, parents aren't very good at this sort of thing. Their anxiety communicates itself to the child and adds to his insecurity. Anxious parents have a way of wanting to check workbooks the minute a child comes home from school. They ask too many questions about what happened in class. They make rules about homework and remedial drills. "Let's be sure you get your work done before there's any playing." Then they get nervous about mistakes: "You *must* know that. You had it yesterday. You're not trying." There may be tears and cross words. The child, already tired from a day of failure, ends up more discouraged than when he started getting "help." Learning becomes more burdensome, rather than easier.

Parents may do better to leave problem-solving to the experts, and concentrate their efforts on making the child's home life relaxing, comfortable, secure—a retreat from the temporary pressure and discomfort of school. When children need remedial work, teachers usually know best what to do. If they can't handle the corrective measures, they can tell parents where to go for help.

The same general advice holds for behavior problems —if and when they should come up. Remember you are going to be upset if you are told that your Suzy—far from being the sweet, lovable, co-operative child you had hoped to produce—is temporarily, at least, a kind of unfriendly, anti-social being. But, try not to jump to conclusions. Avoid the typical parental reaction: Suzy's a flop. Suzy's not going to become the first woman president.

Don't worry about the long-term effects of her five-year-old shortcomings. Try to concentrate on what's behind the trouble and how to right it, now.

The natural reaction is to start nagging and punishing and disapproving. Have you heard excited parents threaten to call off a birthday party, warn a child she won't make friends? Don't be ashamed if you've done such things yourselves, but recognize how counterproductive such tactics are now, and try for something better. What?

Stop, look, and listen—at home and in school, and you'll get some clues to the trouble.

Here are some questions to ask.

The answers will help you figure out what's wrong and how to correct it more effectively than loud-voiced, strong-arm methods.

1. Is your child ever cruel, mean, overbearing at home? If not, is it because you don't allow it? Is he finally breaking loose in school? Or, is he reacting to his first exposure to competition for friends and adult approval?

If you honestly think you're being too tough, ease up on demands and administer extra doses of approval, *when* warranted. If there's not much visible to approve, at the moment, think of assignments you can give that the child will enjoy, so that you *can* reward with praise.

If you're convinced the whole problem started in school, talk to the teacher. Often, listening to a parent gives the teacher a picture of what's going on so that she can help the child settle into school more happily.

Teachers, like parents, often leap to conclusions about a child on skimpy evidence, as if his infractions at age five were signs of an evil nature. If Suzy is mean to Mary, they conclude that Suzy is a spoiled child who needs to be checked. If you explain that Suzy was always kind, playful, easy to reason with, and suggest that she may be a bit frightened by so many children at once, the teacher may feel more protective and also more friendly to Suzy. That may be all Suzy needs.

2. Supposing it is a question of obedience. Polly does as she pleases, the teacher says. If it's time to stop coloring and get out workbooks, Polly goes right on coloring. When her teacher presses her she ignores her completely or says, "I won't," or "You're not my mother." Fighting words for teachers. Supposing every child did as he pleases, they say. Of course every child never would, but the fact is that when one child disobeys, others probably do take the cue. Then it's harder to keep order so children can listen and learn. Besides, a child needs to learn to do what's expected of him or he will have a hard time with children and adults, generally. He won't know how to fit in and listen and learn.

Is his inability to do what he's told recent? Or is it something you've overlooked at home because it didn't bother you, or you didn't think it was serious enough to correct?

If the problem is home-based, what's behind it? Sometimes it's plain neglect. Parents take the easiest way and children do what they like, when they like to. If a teacher complains about the child, the parent will crack down suddenly, issuing rules instead of paying attention. When there isn't immediate compliance, they get very strict and humorless about enforcement. If you think you're in that kind of box, try to get out gracefully. It has no promise. Forget the rules a bit and try laughing, listening, playing, and enjoying your child's company, instead. If you do this, discipline may just happen after a while. The child may not be rebelling at the rules as much as he is showing you his unhappiness at the dreary life that keeps putting him down. When the rules are part of the fabric of a busy, lively, happy, pleasant home, they don't seem too oppressive. They're easier to follow.

Last word: The reactions of a child's teachers and peers sometimes teach him how to get along in life better than your anxious scolding and constant correction. Have confidence in your children. Remember they want to please you and to be like you. The juvenile delinquent of five rarely becomes No. 1 on the FBI's most-wanted list. The underachiever of eight doesn't need to be a college dropout. Children's problems usually get solved even if you make mistakes. You and your child may not be perfect, but he'll come closer to being his best if he's not pushed too hard to be something more than he's capable of at the moment.

5

GIVE YOUR FIRST-GRADER
A GOOD START

First grade is a great big step in a child's life. In first grade, for the first time, children are on their own. Play becomes work. They can tell without marks that results count.

You may be a calm, matter-of-fact parent with total confidence in your five- or six-year-old's ability to make his way in life. Just the same, you will probably have a tickle—too mild for anxiety, maybe, but not quite as pleasant as simple curiosity—about how he will do.

Make no mistake about it, children have similar tremors of anticipation, lightly tinged with terror.

You want your child to get a smooth start. You don't want anything to get in his way. You hope he will start making friends and learning things as quickly as possible. The sooner that happens, the faster his initial misgivings will give way to curiosity, enthusiasm, pride, and confidence. The foundation for becoming a good student and a good playmate will be laid.

In my opinion, the best approach is to take every step

you can to smooth the way before a child starts school, and then let him go—after the first day, of course—by himself, literally and figuratively.

How do you smooth the way? Do you know the school he is going to? Do you know the parents and children who go to it? If you don't, get acquainted. Children are not any kinder, en masse, than they ever were, and the child who stands out in dress or behavior is usually in trouble.

Some day before your child starts in at Theodore Woodrow Garfield, make an appointment, through the principal, and pay a visit. See what first-graders look like, what they wear, and what kind of conduct is customary so you can prepare your child to join the gang.

Last summer friends of my oldest son moved to New York from a semi-rural community where the children's year-round uniform is jeans and T-shirts. The oldest child started first grade soon after the move. She went proudly, the first day, in new blue jeans and a striped T-shirt she had been allowed to pick out herself. She came home crushed. It took her a month to get over the teasing she took. Believe it or not, in this day of woman's lib, the little boys and girls, both, made fun of her for "dressing like a boy."

The wisdom of finding out what the Romans do, and doing accordingly, extends far beyond the simple matter of clothes. A child who uses too big words, knows too many obscure facts, is too well-mannered, too attentive to grown-ups' wishes, too careful about his clothes, or about following rules, can become the target of his schoolmates.

When they are away from home, five-year-olds usually do what their parents have taught them. When schoolmates laugh, they don't know what's funny, or how to get in step.

Children who have spent more time with grown-ups than with boys and girls their own age are the ones most likely to seem "different" to their peers. "Different" is just about the hardest thing to be in first grade. If you don't know the neighborhood, get acquainted. Some schools have an orientation session before school starts, for first-graders and their parents. But, if you don't know any of the teachers or parents, it might even be a good idea to arrange a visit to the school the spring before your child begins. Watching the children and talking to parents and teachers can give you the feel of the place and some idea of what grown-ups and children, both, expect of beginners.

The children may seem loud, rough, and a bit too inconsiderate of the grown-ups around them. You may consider their language rude, crude, or sloppy. Good thing to find out! Good idea for your prospective first-grader to get a little initiation. If he cringes, reassure him. More likely, however, he'll find the children's high spirits and exuberance exciting, and be eager to join the fun. You'll be tempted to pull back, be disapproving. But, no matter what critical, clucking noises stir within you, bite your tongue. Much better to let a child find his way in new surroundings with no strings attached, than to make him fearful and self-conscious about his classmates before he even knows them.

You can assume that even a six-year-old will be as aware of the contrast between school and home standards as you are. If he overreacts to their ways and goes on a tear for a while, let it happen. After he is set you will have no trouble restoring your rules at home.

If your family has a casual, informal style of life,

your child might have a problem adapting to more demanding standards that prevail at school. Help him accept the rules of the road easily. Refrain from doing or saying anything that would give him the idea that you disapprove of his teacher's demands. Johnny may have to join his thirty-five classmates each morning, fold his hands on the same spot on his desk with everyone else, and say at a signal from teacher, "Good morning, Miss Blue." You may think this is the silliest, most time-wasting exercise imaginable. Keep it to yourself. It's much easier for Johnny to do what everyone else is doing and feel he is part of the gang, than to get out of step with teacher and friends by clowning around or disrupting, because you've made him feel what his teacher wants is silly.

If you think your child will become hopelessly confused by having to follow one set of rules at school and another at home, forget it. Children, being human, are almost infinitely adaptable. They accept, as natural, the fact that teachers may say one thing and parents another. The only thing that *does* confuse them is when you break down the teacher's authority by making fun of her or her methods.

If you want your child to concentrate on the main work of first grade—settling in and *learning to learn*—don't give him conflicting signals. Find out what the teacher expects and use your own authority to teach him to respect his teacher's.

Don't make the mistake of many concerned, well-informed parents, and argue about the teacher's methods with spouses, relatives, and friends, where your child can hear.

You may think you know best how to run this particular first grade class, but keep your discussions private, and make clear to your child, from the start, that teachers are to be obeyed.

One of the most important lessons to learn in first grade is how to follow instructions. If a child thinks you disapprove of his teacher, he will be all mixed up. He won't know whether to follow her directions, entertain his neighbor while she's giving them, or ignore them completely.

There may be a dozen different ways for a first grade teacher to establish discipline—one as effective and valid as another. It is one thing for a mother to manage one first-grader, plus a sibling or two, in the hours when she is in full command, and another for a teacher to establish constant control over twenty-five or thirty-five children so that they can learn what's expected with a certain amount of efficiency, equanimity, and enjoyment.

Some teachers who seem almost inhumanly demanding of first-graders set high standards purposely during the first weeks of school because they have found that children settle down more easily and quickly when they know just what is expected. Then, when order and organization are established, these teachers can practically forget about commands, speeches, rewards, and punishment. If the teacher makes work reasonably interesting, children go at it busily and happily.

Propagate your own philosophy and family values at home, among friends. At school, support the teacher who is in charge. In the long run your children will probably adopt the philosophy and values they learn from you and your friends. It is not worth while, usually, to fight for your point of view with teachers. You run the risk of mixing your child up about whom to listen to in the classroom, without gaining much for him.

We are apt to forget that children have lots to learn before they can make it alone in the world, and in order to learn it as easily and happily as possible they have to be able to trust the grown-ups around them who are their teachers. Teachers make mistakes like everyone else, but I have found very few who are actually anti-children.

If they are, of course, you have to take action. First-graders aren't always completely articulate about things that bother them. If they know they're supposed to get along well in school, they may be hesitant about complaining. Nevertheless, you can usually tell when something is wrong. Your child will show signs of wilting. His attitude at home will change in some clear way. He won't eat. He may feel sick in the morning. He will be tired and cross after school, or mean to his cat or dog —if he has one—or to his dolls if he plays house. If questioned, he may complain directly that his teacher doesn't like him, is mean, makes the children laugh at him, and so on. If you see these signs, I think you should make an appointment with the child's teacher, report what you have noticed, and find out what's going on in class. You may get a call from the teacher, even before you've noticed anything wrong yourself.

What do teachers do that is anti-child? They single out one or two children and make scapegoats of them. They resort to sarcasm or ridicule to put a child down or they turn the rest of the class against him.

I remember one of our children regaling us at dinner with imitations of his teacher. After every explanation she'd say, "Now I know you all know just what I want you to do—that is all but —— tell me, class, who is the *one* child who never listens?" And the class would chorus, "Jimmy."

One of my friends asked her second-grader why she was so cross after school and the child said, "You would be, too, if your teacher called you STUPID all day in front of your friends."

Naturally my friend made an appointment with the teacher, who complained that the seven-year-old didn't listen, didn't remember instructions, and kept running to her desk for help all day long. She volunteered that she was so tired of telling my friend's daughter to stop talking to the girl behind her that she finally turned the child's desk around so she wouldn't have to twist backward to keep in touch with her friend. Finally, the teacher said to my friend, "You know I can't be her mother."

Totally unintimidated, my friend said, "But that's just what you have to be with second-graders a good deal of the time. They are very young. Maybe if you gave her more attention she would *pay* more attention to you."

The teacher remained silent. My friend knew that she had made no impression and that nothing would change. Since it was close to the end of the school year she didn't go to the principal and ask to have her daughter moved to another class. Instead she told her child that some teachers are fussier than others and all you can do is make the best of it. She advised her to be as pleasant as possible and try to pay more attention. Then, to counter the teacher's dampening influence, she gave her as much praise and attention as possible at home, and reminded her, more than once, that it would pay to do her best in the last weeks of school so she would be ready for the third grade teacher, whom they both knew—from an older brother's reports—was "really neat."

Next year there was no trouble whatever.

If you hear or see that a child is getting a rough deal from a teacher don't hesitate to take it up with her. If that doesn't help, go to the principal. Any halfway decent principal will do anything she can to prevent a child from developing a school phobia. You have a right to ask that your child be transferred to another class, if you have reasonably good evidence that he is not getting a fair deal from the teacher he has. If you can't do anything, do your best to support the child at home. Make sure you don't blame him for his teacher's mistake, and thereby reinforce her destructive effect.

Now for the other side of the coin. Believe it or not, teachers are often more fearful of parents than parents are of them. It is therefore helpful to them, and valuable for your children, to establish easy, friendly relations early in the game.

Find out before school opens, or make a point of asking the teacher during the first week of school, what she expects of parents and children. Then make sure your child understands her rules. Put them to him simply and directly: "You must not talk to other children when Miss Blue is talking to the class." Or, "You must be careful not to disturb anyone else or interfere with his work." "Try hard to do what Miss Blue says just as if she were Daddy or me. Listen. Follow directions. That's the way to learn."

In talking to the teacher, find out what she expects you to do at home. Does she give homework? How much does she expect done? Does she want you to explain or help when asked? If the child doesn't understand what to do, does she expect you to show him?

Let her know you will always make yourself available if she wants to talk to you or enlist your help.

Mothers and fathers who work, as I always have,

can't arrange conferences with teachers easily. No parent, however, is so rushed that he cannot manage a few minutes before or after school to keep in touch with the teacher. I always gave each of my children's teachers a card with both their parents' names and phone numbers and a note about the best times to reach each of us. I always reinforced this with an underlined message: "Call us any time you have a question."

I remember once getting an urgent call from one of the children's first grade teachers asking me to stop in when I dropped the children off the next morning. When I got there the child's teacher quickly told me there was nothing to report. She was simply making a test case for my son. The day before, she had corrected him with the remark, "If you have to be reminded about this much longer I think I'll have to talk to your mother." The child answered, in effect, "You can't talk to my mother. She's too busy to come here."

The teacher wanted the child to know that he was up against a united parent-teacher front, so she called for me. I was glad that she had. There were no further incidents. She had established her authority and I had helped assure our child that his parents were friendly allies with her—although not *against* him. A teacher who is fearful of talking to a parent about an incipient problem puts it off. By the time she decides something has to be done it is often too late. The problem is out of hand. Then the parent is critical of the teacher for delaying. But while her criticism may be justified, it won't correct the damage that has been done the child. If you can make a teacher comfortable with you at the start of each school year, you can be much more certain to get the important bulletins you should have on your child's progress—good or bad—when appropriate.

It is amazing how often parents fail to establish a cordial relationship with their children's teachers. When this happens, one party or both parties are on the defensive and the relationship breaks down easily over the sensitive subject of a child's academic or social behavior. Parents can be fierce as tigers when they think their young are threatened. It's not a bit unusual for a mother to react to a teacher's innocent question as if it were an attack.

For example, a teacher asks a parent, "Can you give me some help about getting Richard to listen more closely to my instructions?"

The mother, instead of listening to the teacher, ignores her question completely and gives this bristly non-answer. "Richie must be bored." Which is, of course, the same as saying to the teacher, "You're boring. You can't teach my child."

If there were as many bored first-graders as parents report, most first year, first grade teachers would never get a second chance.

I have seen my share of these bored children, brought to me by parents who want their own diagnoses verified. More often than not the children are not bored, but lost, because they have never learned to follow instructions and do what is expected. You can see how they become inattentive and unadjusted. Their parents have made them feel that everyone else is out of step. The children are waiting for the world to fit them.

I can say, quite dogmatically, that very few children are so advanced, sensitive, singular, or creative that first grade work bores them—assuming that the teacher allows each child the individual leeway that is reasonable.

Even if you have the rare exception who is really

marking time in first grade, it is counterproductive, in my opinion, to respond to a teacher's efforts to discuss the child by rushing to his defense. Instead, ask her to describe his behavior and tell you what she thinks about it. Ask her advice; then tell her, if you are ready, how her report of the child jibes with your own experience at home. This has several advantages as a course of action. It lets her know that you appreciate her interest and respect her judgment and take her seriously. It gives you a chance to evaluate what she says and respond intelligently, instead of reacting blindly. It keeps the door open so that she can call on you for help in the future.

It is, by the way, not necessary for you to react finally, on the spot, at all. Far better to discuss the problem, tell her what you think, tentatively; then watch what goes on at home in the light of what you've talked about; discuss the problem with your husband or wife; then talk to the teacher again.

After all this you may decide the teacher has pointed out a very obvious shortcoming in your child. Maybe you'll decide you have been careless about seeing that he pays attention and does what he is told at home. Then you will be able to make corrections while he is still very young and you will be grateful that a first grade teacher was interested enough to help.

If you decide that your child is really not sufficiently challenged by first grade, there will still be time to raise this issue with the teacher. Do it by asking questions instead of by leveling criticism. First ask whether your child is keeping up with the class. If he is, you might say, pleasantly, "I'm surprised that he doesn't pay attention. He seems to be so curious and interested in everything when he's with us. While I was at the library committee meeting last week he and Allison dug up a little space and planted a vegetable garden with my seeds. They'd done it all exactly right. I asked him how they knew how to do it and he said, 'I just remembered how Daddy did his last week.'"

No teacher is likely to be antagonized by that. And no halfway perceptible teacher could fail to get the message: a child who is that attentive at home needs more stimulation in school. A good teacher might reply without any more discussion, "Perhaps I should give Josh [or Kate or Bill] more responsibility than I do. I'm going to try that."

From all the above it may sound as if I believe teachers are always right and parents are usually wrong; or that parents should make teachers feel that they are right even if they don't believe it. You may also think I favor the homogenized child with "slipeez" plasticity.

Quite the contrary, I believe that parents' values, views, convictions, taste, standards, should always come first. But I also believe that medium-good parents' standards always do prevail in the long run. I feel this so strongly that I don't think it important enough to make an issue of *you* versus *them* with a five-year-old child, except when your child is being victimized—as I have described above.

If you find a school and its philosophy and methods so completely contrary to what you consider good and necessary for your child's proper development, then move him. If you think the school he's going to is passing fair, go along easily. As I've said, teaching a child to get along with his peers and his teachers will not break down family standards and influence in the long run. It will make him a lot happier getting started.

It may sound ridiculous, but the last thing I'd like to talk about is academic preparation. Many children have trouble because they do not know what they are expected to, or are temperamentally unable to use their knowledge. An illustration came from a mother we talked to in Massachusetts a few weeks after her fifth child started first grade. The teacher reported that she was falling behind because she didn't understand English. Maria's mother couldn't believe it. She spoke German to her children, but their father talked to them in English. Since none of their other children had had school problems, she had assumed they were fluent bilinguists. What she had forgotten, however, was that Maria was temperamentally entirely different from her brothers and sisters. None of the children had been fluent in English. The rest had caught on quickly because they were outgoing and gregarious, and not afraid to ask questions. Maria was shy and retiring. The less she understood the harder it was to ask for help.

Fortunately—in a sense—she got sick. When she was well several weeks later, her smart parents decided to keep her home for the rest of the year. Her mother stopped talking to her in German, and gave her a chance to catch up socially. She started first grade again the following fall and did just fine.

This illustrates two things about preparing your children for school. First, make sure that they know what their teacher expects them to know, and second, do whatever you can to help them overcome or control the temperamental qualities that might make school hard for them.

Children usually pick up all the academic background they need, as I have listed it above, from parents and older brothers and sisters. If not, they learn it in nursery school or kindergarten. However, it won't hurt to check with the school your child is to attend, ahead of time. Find out what they want first graders to know at the start and, without pushing it, make certain your child goes prepared.

The temperamental question is not that easy. However, if you are aware that temperamental traits can affect a child's ability to adjust to school, and to learning, you may be able to modify them somewhat in the preschool period.

The most troublesome traits are excessive shyness related to lack of ability to change and accept new situations, and excessive activity related to high distractibility and short span of attention.

If you have a highly active, or shy, or restless child, or one who has a very hard time going into new groups of people, or sitting still long enough to let you read a story or put on snowsuits and so on, you have probably been attempting to temper his temperament ever since he was a baby. At the same time, he has probably tempered yours, too, so that you automatically have adjusted your demands somewhat to fit him. You don't treat him the way you do your other children who have less marked traits. You accept more moving around, less attentiveness. You offer more support to the shy child. I want to suggest that you make a conscious effort when a child of this sort is three or four, to begin to train him to adapt to the world around him, so that he will not get in his own way too much when he starts school.

How do you do it? By making demands consistent with a child's ability to comply, and then seeing that he does. The mistake most parents make with children who are harder to handle than the average, is to lay down demands that they simply cannot meet. For instance, parents of highly active, energetic, distractible children often treat them as if they were average. Their demands may be reasonable, but not for such children. When the child fails to meet them parents nag, give up, get mad, vacillate, punish. The child gets cross, confused, feels abused, doesn't get anywhere. Much better to ask for what's possible and then see that you get it. Then the child feels he's pleasing. You and he don't get into a battle of wills. He has an incentive really to try to learn what to do. You won't change his temperament, but you'll keep him on your side, trying to conform. As he gets older time itself will help temper his temperament if he doesn't get sidetracked into fighting for his way.

Let's look at a three-year-old who can't sit still for meals. Figure out what is possible. Let's say you know he can last through meat and vegetables, if he wants to. Then say, "You must sit with us until you finish what you want. Then run and play and we'll call you for dessert."

Give him several trial runs, then see that he keeps the agreement. If he gets up ahead of time, clear away his plate.

Try not to be too earnest about it. Let it be a game—half fun, but also serious. Don't start until the child is old enough to understand the rules and able to begin to comply, and don't try to change everything at once. If and when you succeed in one area, move on to another, until the child begins to appreciate what he can do. I think you can see how valuable this kind of preparatory training is when a child starts school and has to pay attention, sit still, and apply what he is learning.

Suppose you have a shy child. I think you should begin in the toddler years—three and four—exposing him to new people and scenes without demanding much of him. The very fact of being present with you and absorbing your social know-how is some help. If he spends the whole time clinging, O.K. The next step is to arrange for him to play around other children regularly—even if he is not actually engaged with them. In the playground, in day care groups, children learn to feel comfortable with other children, long before they play together. Even if a child is fearful of the sandbox or of the swings in the park, I would keep taking him regularly so that he learns from experience that there is nothing to be afraid of. I would also start asking other children to play at home, even if your child plays in a corner hugging most of his toys to himself at first. I would also take him to other children's houses to play when possible, staying, if necessary, until you know he can recognize the other child's mother, but after that, expecting him to be alone for short periods.

Finally, before he starts school I would take him to visit and talk with the teacher two or three times.

I don't want to give you the idea that you can change a child's temperament, because I don't believe you can. What you can do is help children modify their behavior so that they will adjust to school more quickly and be able to learn more effectively. We don't want to turn out homogenized kids. In fact, most of us hope to teach our children to adapt to differences in human beings—not only differences of background, but differences of personality, intelligence, and temperament. Part of one's success in helping a child adapt to the demands of any group—school, play, sport, music, whatever—comes from appreciating his individuality enough to know how much he can bend. So, while you take a shy child to school ahead of time so that he can get used to the teacher and the room and the routine that is expected, you also should try to explain his nature to his teacher so that she can respond to him in a helpful rather than a punitive way. If I had an excessively shy child, I might want to warn the teacher that he sometimes masks his shyness by pretending he is not listening—simply to avoid being called on. Knowing that might keep her from scolding him. It might also influence her to find painless ways of drawing him into the group.

There are just a few more precautions to take to make sure a child is ready for grade one. They concern physical health. I can't tell you how many parents have told me about children who failed during the first two or three years of school before their parents or teachers discovered that they couldn't hear, or couldn't see the blackboard.

You may not believe it, but this story was told us by the family to whom it happened. The mother took her first child to kindergarten; she asked about eye and hearing tests. She was told the school took care of all that. She offered to take the child to her pediatrician to have the tests made. The teacher assured her it was unnecessary. In third grade the child's teacher suggested a hearing test. The child, by then, was two years behind her classmates in reading. The test revealed that her hearing was so badly impaired that she could not possibly have heard the teacher from where she was sitting. After an operation she began to catch up. In fifth grade—after four years of unhappiness and failure—she is doing well and blossoming.

The story could be repeated again and again—about hearing, about faulty vision, and also about language problems—unrelated to a non-English-speaking background.

Here is another story, about a nursery school child. The child hardly spoke, looked blank. Everyone thought she was retarded. The psychologist found she was perfectly bright, but had a slight language lag. She needed more time and practice than other children her age to understand and assimilate what she heard. And she was also a slow talker. This unimportant difference had been exaggerated by the way her family treated her. They had decided she was backward when she was all of two years old and had stopped talking to her. In addition, they referred to her constantly as stupid. As a result, her natural difficulty had been complicated by confusion, fear, and shame. The school director talked to her parents, explained the effect of what they were doing, and suggested proper corrective measures. The parents changed when they recognized what they had done. The little girl began to respond, smile, talk, and brighten up. She will be normal by first grade, the psychologist says.

If you notice that your child is slow to speak or understand, don't ignore it. Take the necessary precautions and follow the advice you get, as outlined in Chapter Fourteen.

Most language lags can be handled perfectly well at home once all concerned know what is needed. Teachers, of course, should be kept informed and instructed about what they can do to help.

One last suggestion. Apparently, many parents are so busy teaching the alphabet, reading readiness, and elementary math, that they forget to show their fledgling scholars how to tie their shoes, blow their noses, button their coats, zip up, and remember to hang on to at least some of their belongings. I can't tell you how many teachers in the schools Jane Whitbread and I visited begged us to remind parents to teach their children the fundamentals of taking care of themselves before they start school. Teachers, of course, have a lot more time to teach when their children are minimally self-supporting.

CHAPTER FIVE

Q & A

Q. How can you tell when children are having a hard time with their schoolwork?

A. Most first-graders like to pretend they have homework. After the first weeks of school, teachers often give them simple assignments to do at home to make them feel "grown-up." There may be a few words to learn, a page of a workbook to do, or a preprimer to read from. When your child brings work home you will probably be curious enough about what he is learning to ask to see what he is doing, and he will be proud enough to want to show you.

You can judge his progress from the way he proceeds. If everything is all right, he will know just what he is supposed to do and you will see that he does it easily. If, for example, he has a list of words, he may have to ask your help at first. But after you have told him the new words two or three times he will be able to say them correctly. If he has a primer to read from, he will know where to begin and where to stop, and he will know some, if not all, of the words. If he has something to do in his workbook, he will remember the instructions. He may need to ask you a question or two but you will see that he understands in general what he is supposed to do and how to do it.

These are signs that the work is hard: 1. He will *not* be eager to show you what he is doing. 2. He will be fuzzy about what he is supposed to do. For example, he may think he is supposed to copy the words—which is unlikely—instead of learn them. He may not have the vaguest notion of where he is supposed to work in his workbook, or what the work is. 3. He may not know any words in his primer. Of course you would not expect a child to know every word. He is in school to learn. But, if he acts as if his book were completely new to him, and does not remember any of the simple words, even after you have told them to him several times, he is obviously not getting on very well.

Q. If you think a child is having trouble what should you do?

A. Don't show concern or alarm to the child. If he shows you his work, simply answer his questions, help him along, and refrain from negative comments like, "I just told you." "You must remember that." "Don't you listen to your teacher?"

The person to take your worries to is the teacher. Make an appointment to see her. She may tell you everything is slow but normal. She may suggest waiting to see whether your child's lag is temporary. She may give you simple drills to practice at home that will help him listen better, so that he can remember instructions, ask the proper questions about what he does not understand, in class, and so on.

Q. Do you think first-graders should have homework that interferes with their playtime?

A. Absolutely not. If teachers give homework that takes most of the class more than fifteen minutes or half an hour, I would suggest that she shorten the assignments. If the child enjoys doing homework and spends more time on it, by choice, I would not interfere. However, if the extra time is spent copying and recopying in order to produce completely pristine and perfect work I would try to curb his excess zeal. Children need to be able to distinguish between pride in work and pointless perfectionism that may actually prevent concentration on content.

You must have his teacher's support for your campaign. If you think a child is being too fussy, and he insists he is only doing what his teacher told him to, check with her before you tell him he is overdiligent. Ask her support, too, in persuading him to spend less time on details of content and appearance and more on understanding and thinking.

Q. Isn't it silly to give first-graders homework after a five-hour school day?

A. A school day is more than enough time, even with interruptions for collecting milk money, giving out papers, and stretching between periods. But brief homework does serve a purpose. It gives parents a chance to see what is going on and how a child is getting along. It gives children a chance to enjoy the fruits of their labor and their parents' approval. It also establishes the habit of homework, painlessly. All this can be accomplished in other ways, too. Many teachers don't bother with homework in first grade, but it certainly does no harm.

Q. My child gets so upset she cannot sleep the night before tests. What can I do to make her less of a worrier?

A. First find out why she is so anxious. Does the teacher put too much stress on tests? If so, you will find out by talking with other mothers in the class, some of whose children, at least, will be worrying, too. Point this out to the teacher and see if you can't persuade her to be less intense.

Is it the result of poor preparation? Is she worried because she really doesn't understand the work? If so—and your child's teacher can answer that question—you naturally will want to see how to help her do better.

Is she by nature abnormally anxious? If so, your decision about whether to seek professional help would hinge on whether her anxiety is diminishing, gradually, as she grows; and whether it interferes with her school and social adjustment. If it keeps her from listening and absorbing what she is being taught, and from thinking clearly on tests, I would recommend help.

GROWTH AND LEARNING

Last week I was watching a friend play tennis. Her two-and-a-half-year-old daughter was on the sidelines, alternately rolling in the grass, watching the game, edging on to the court and being shooed away, eying me (a stranger), and whining. Eventually whining predominated.

First her mother ignored it. Then she said, "Stop it. We're playing."

Finally she became severe. "You asked to come, remember? You promised to be good. Now be still."

The little girl did pretty well, but her mother didn't deserve such good fortune. She was indulging in a fantasy common to parents, from the beginning of time. She was pretending that her daughter was a great deal older than her years and capable of things a two-year-old could not begin to understand.

Ever hear a father say to a sobbing three-year-old, "Come on, now. Stop crying. Don't act like a baby." As if he *weren't* a baby. As if he could possibly muster the kind of constant self-control the father tries to exhibit.

When a two-year-old says, "I wanna come," and her

mother says, "You know there's nothing to do there. You'll just have to sit." And the child says, "I wanna come." And the mother says, "Promise then you won't bother me?" And the child shakes her head vigorously in the affirmative, it means one thing: "I wanna come."

A two-year-old knows only what he or she wants at the moment. After ten minutes in the hot sun with the bugs biting, watching a grown-up game, and not being able to say anything, or get any attention, she wants to go home. She cannot understand promises. She has a short memory, and little conception of time. She lives in the moment, guided more or less completely by her own feelings.

This two-year-old stayed. But the level of her physiological, emotional, and mental development all conspired to prevent her from learning anything from the experience. The same scene could repeat itself a hundred times before she is five or six with very little change in her reactions. At this age, a child simply hasn't the capacity to weigh the pleasure of being with her mother against the future agony of being with her, *but* deprived of her attention. The mind cannot grasp. The senses cannot remember.

Her parents, like all parents, will probably go right on yielding impulsively to her wishes even as they realize they are courting disaster. In this instance, the disaster is minor—a little distraction from the game. The child is reminded foolishly of her promise, mildly chastised, not really blamed. At the end she is comforted, restored to good spirits. All is forgotten until the next time.

I have told this story, however, because there *are* times and places when ignoring a child's developmental capacity can be destructive, particularly when it gets to be a habit. Americans tend to push children on to ever better performance in school, just as we push our machines on the production line. However, we are not as tolerant and understanding when children don't deliver as we are when the machines break down.

I think it is important to let your children know you consider schoolwork important. I do not advocate abandoning your parental prerogative to urge children to do their best. But there is a universal timetable for human development that limits children's capacity from day to day. Children will try harder and be more successful if you are careful to set goals for them they can realistically meet, considering their individual rates of development and learning styles.

When a child of any age says "I can't" or "I don't understand," take it at face value. Children are not naturally lazy, deceitful, contrary, or indifferent to their parents' wishes. They like to please parents. Approval is nicer than disapproval. "I can't" means that a child is physically, mentally, emotionally, or temperamentally sure, at the moment, that he can't. So, stop before you react to a child's performance, lack of performance, refusal to perform, or plea for help and ask yourself a few questions:

"Isn't David doing the best he can right now? Why don't I let him know that instead of pushing him harder?"

"Why should I hurry Jill to do her homework faster, as long as she does finish and seems to enjoy doing it?"

"Are we being too strict with Stevie? Is that why he loses all his assignments and tests?"

"Is Sally charming her teacher into thinking she understands when she doesn't? Have we taught her that pleasing people comes first?"

"Aren't we wrong to tell Freddy not to let his teacher bother him? Why shouldn't a seven-year-old be upset when the grown-up he's with all day picks on him?"

Consider your child's age and the level of development that should be appropriate, then adjust it for his individual pace and style. Intellect, understanding, and the ability to learn develop gradually as the result of many complex interacting factors. Probably physiological development is the most central influence. There has to be capacity before there can be performance. A child has to see, hear, experience his senses, and gain some control over his muscles before he can begin to get things together. At first he can barely see the bottle that gives him milk. In a few weeks he can see and touch it and suck, all at once. Some months later he can hold it, suck, remove it, look at it, put it back. He has not only learned to connect hand, eye, mouth, and bottle, he has also stored in his senses, muscles, and mind information that he can apply to more sophisticated tasks later.

How he will apply this information depends on his environment; the opportunities it offers for experiment; and the expectations it sets for him. But, whether he is a primitive child in an agricultural society or a city child surrounded by all kinds of mechanical and electronic wizardry, he can only understand so much at a given age in his early life. If he is good at remembering, he may be able to give the right answers, but he cannot use them until he knows what they mean. For example, a six-month-old baby, while perfectly able to tell the difference between objects of various shapes, is unable to fit them into the right-shaped holes, no matter how diligently you practice with him. A three-year-old will tell you that the leaves on the trees move "because they blow." You can teach a child at this age to say, "The wind blows them," but if you or someone else asks tomorrow, he will revert to his own view, "They blow," as if some internal device programs him to see it that way. Then suddenly, just as immutably, four or five years later if you ask him again, he will say, "The wind blows them."

A five-year-old might count to twelve, but if you line twelve apples in two rows—one longer than the other—and ask which row has more apples he'll invariably point to the longer. He will insist—even after counting six in each row—that there are more in the line that is longer. At age seven, apparently automatically, his answer changes to the correct one. It's almost as if children have to experience and ponder reality for a certain time and with certain ever-growing powers to perceive and conceive, before reality is clear to them. And this unfolds in orderly sequence for all children at roughly the same ages.

The development of social behavior, ideas about right and wrong, and emotional control all develop in the same fashion, limited by physiological growth and control and influenced by the demands of the environment.

Babies and small children, almost totally helpless to cope with their world, depend on mothers and fathers and other adults to keep them safe and comfortable. Obviously, the approval of those on whom they depend for life itself is very important to them.

In their restricted existence they have neither the experience nor the understanding to see the world from other people's view. They are guided almost entirely by their own needs and wants.

Gradually, as a child moves out into the world and becomes more independent, his self-centered view changes and he can see the difference between himself and others; recognize other people's needs and wants; share and understand; follow rules. Partly as a by-product of his increasing socialization, he begins to develop a clear picture of himself as a person with a past, present, and future. He makes friends, develops interests that suit him. He starts to think ahead and to imagine what he will be and do as an adult.

Children's growth patterns will vary according to their individual capacities and rates of growth and the temperamental qualities they were born with.

How can you master all this information about development, so that your expectations will be realistic? You don't need to. In fact, even if you were an expert in development, familiar with the characteristics of each growth stage from birth to fifteen years, knowing your own child would be more helpful to you. His growing up, while it follows a general pattern, bears his own stamp. No one can read it for you. You recognize it by being with him and watching him from his very early days. You probably know, even without his words, what he is able to do and when he is overwhelmed; how he can learn best; what kinds of things confuse him. All you need to know about development are the general capacities and limitations of his age group. The rest comes from knowing your child.

Perhaps that sounds simpler than it is. Be sure you *are* watching and listening to him and not blindly making him the tool of your wish for a brilliant student. I mention this because I see so many children who suffer from their parents' insistence that they are something that they are not. Actually, they are just average good kids until their parents' hopeless expectations mix them up. Not very long ago I was introduced to a ten-year-old boy, described by his mother as a brilliant scientist. She wanted me to have his school transfer him to the gifted class, although they had told her he was not yet reading at grade level.

We began to talk about his interests. He wanted to tell me all about the structure of the atom. Very impressive. We began discussing. He drew me a diagram and I asked him what the various parts of the picture represented. He had memorized the names—proton, neutron, nucleus. He spouted chemical formulas, but he hadn't the slightest notion of how chemical changes take place. He began to feel nervous when he couldn't answer my questions and adroitly changed the subject to his other "fields of interest," which he identified as paleontology, zoology, and other rather esoteric "ologies" for a ten-year-old to absorb. I asked what paleontology was. He didn't know. This perfectly bright child was being encouraged by his parents to be a non-learner. By force feeding his agile memory, his parents were persuading themselves and him to think that he was much beyond learning the very basic tools that might eventually help him become the brilliant scientist they wanted him to be—assuming of course that that was what *he* wanted to be.

Keep this quite extreme case in mind the next time a child comes to you with a puzzled look and says, "I can't understand. Help me." Help him where he is—not where you want him to be.

If your eight-year-old comes home from school and tells you his back hurts, you know just how to help him. You ask if anything happened to make it hurt. You look at the sore place. You try different remedies—rubbing, hot compresses, cold compresses, a heating pad, aspirin. You keep asking whether your treatment helps. You keep assuring him it will surely get better in a day or so.

When a child says, "I don't understand," use this same approach. Try to help. Find out what he doesn't understand. Try to explain. Ask whether your explanation is helping. Assure him you know he'll understand if you and he both keep trying. Don't be impatient. Don't question his effort, his attentiveness, his past, present, or future behavior. Deal with facts. He does not understand. He is eight years old. You may wish he was quicker, more conscientious, more determined. You may wonder why he isn't as relaxed a learner as his older sister or brother, and wonder what you or he did or did not do to make him that way. But that won't help. What helps is paying attention to the way he is developing and sticking to the matter at hand; solving his problem of the moment to his satisfaction.

Suppose you had a child who was a year old and not yet walking—even though his nine-month-old cousin was running all over the place. You wouldn't stand your child on a wall and tell him to jump just to get him started; then get angry when he cried and said "no"; tell him he was stupid for not trying; warn him that he would never learn to walk if he didn't hurry up, etc.

Understanding and learning develop in an orderly manner just the way physical maturity does. And no matter how much you want to hurry them up they have to proceed in their orderly sequence; and then only after experience and practice have engraved them in the mind and made them automatic. Each successive advance in seeing and understanding follows from the preceding one the way walking follows a tentative wobbling stance and tottering first steps. Walking must become automatic before a child can think about jumping.

Meet the need of the moment. If you do that, you will work with the child's own developmental timetable and pattern. It is not just a matter of setting a realistic goal rather than an impossible one. More important, it is getting on the child's side, letting him have the support from you that is essential for an eight-year-old's steady development. If you expect him to learn he thinks he can and thinking helps to make it so. It gives him the will to try. Your expectations and his teachers' tell him what is possible for him. He cannot judge for himself. He needs your approval to urge him on until he is old enough (twelve to fourteen) to judge his own abilities independently.

A very interesting study was made in California a few years ago. It showed that even mediocre students can exceed themselves when their teachers' expectations are high.

A team of investigators went into a ghetto school and tested the students for academic potential. Then, ignoring their scores, they divided the students into two groups in a scientifically determined, random fashion. They identified one group to the teachers as late bloomers, whose academic promise would be realized in the year at hand.

Lo and behold, at the end of the year it came to pass. This group—exactly comparable with their classmates— as far as could be scientifically established, far outshone them. Their teachers expected them to succeed. The children got the message, plus extra attention from the teachers. It gave them confidence and will and they came through. Children who still have not developed a clear image of themselves live up to the image important adults project for them.

Between the ages of eight and twelve or thirteen they make immense progress in understanding how the world works; the relation between cause and effect; the rules for social conduct, etc. By early adolescence, they are capable of learning as much as they ever will be. As they mature intellectually, they are reaching their maximum physical development. The two kinds of growth are closely interdependent all along.

By the age of twelve to fourteen, they are strong. They have seen the world (more or less). They have had enough experience to be able to predict what will happen, given a certain set of circumstances or sequence of events. This gives them the satisfying feeling that they can cope on their own. They don't need their mothers and fathers and teachers as much as they used to. They begin to see themselves continuing on into the future—grown up. They think about what they want to be and to do and imagine how it would feel. Now they have reason to learn for themselves—not for teachers and parents. While the first important adults in their lives will always influence them—even when silent—there is a difference.

You expect your eight-year-old to be upset if his teacher picks on him. When a twelve-year-old comes home from school boiling with tales of injustice and cruelty and says, "I'm not going to study for that old witch," you know he can quite well separate his own interests from the need for his teacher's approval. You can say, "If she's so rotten, why let her stop you from learning algebra. Don't you need it if you want to be an engineer?" It won't make him like the teacher but he'll get the point.

To sum it all up, if you take care that your expectations and efforts to help are consistent with your child's abilities at any given stage of development, you'll support his progress to the next level of intellectual and social maturity in the most effective way.

CHAPTER SIX

Q & A

Q. One of my children has a fantastic grasp of ecology even though he is only five. The other day I found myself reasoning with him as if he were at least ten about the moral issues involved in "making up" stories to impress or frighten his little brother. Later I realized that he couldn't possibly understand emotionally what I was talking about. Can you suggest any guidelines to help me know what to expect?

A. Children often have an amazing grasp of certain kinds of factual material and seem very sophisticated, when their intellectual and emotional development are still at a very primitive level. This can mislead adults into expecting judgment and behavior that are beyond them.

Following rules, observing social niceties, respecting private property, telling the truth, and many other kinds of behavior depend on the ability to evaluate situations, make judgments, abstract the general from the particular, and apply the particular to the general. These capacities evolve with over-all development, experience, instruction, and practice. Here is a timetable to give you an idea of what to expect of children at various stages of growth. The ages given are approximate, since the rate of development can vary widely from child to child.

OBEYING RULES

Ages 1–2 Can obey simple commands, on the spot. He can understand and obey "Don't touch the lamp," but he can't remember. You have to keep telling him. If you leave the room, the rule leaves his head.

As he begins to get old enough to remember the rule he will test his memory, and your seriousness, by touching the lamp over and over and waiting for you to say "no."

Ages 2–4 Probably can remember a few important rules. Generally can keep his hands off prized family possessions; will regress to earlier behavior when tired, cross, frustrated, or sick.

TELLING THE TRUTH

Ages 1–4 Does not know true from false. If he breaks the lamp and you hear the crash, come running, and say, "Did you touch the lamp?" he'll say, "No." He will remember the rule when he sees you, the rule giver, and he will answer "No," to please, just as he will answer "Yes," to please, if you say "Do you love me?"

Ages 4–5 He begins to know right from wrong, true from false. If you have taught him not to pull the cat's tail he will not. But he cannot discriminate, or generalize. If he sees two or three of his friends teasing a cat in the schoolyard he will join the fun. If you scold him and say, "You know better than to tease a cat," he may say, "I didn't tease our cat." He is not trying to rationalize. He is simply still unable to generalize "Don't tease animals" from the particular rule "Don't tease our cat."

Ages 5–8 He now understands rules absolutely. This is a very strict, self-righteous age. He will remind you, when you don't toe the line. "You didn't brush your teeth after breakfast." He may tattle on classmates. "Sara is eating the icing on the birthday cake," a five-year-old will tell the mother of the hostess at the birthday party.

Children get into endless fights about rules when they play games. They will turn down your help if your ways differ even slightly from the teacher's. If your sevens don't look like hers you may be rejected. There is only one right way and it belongs to the putative authority in the case. It seems as if the slightest deviation would undermine the whole structure of the child's universe.

Ages 8–9 He is beginning to develop judgment. He can make exceptions to rules, using his own conscience and judgment about when it is appropriate. He may, for example, decide to go outdoors for his football in December, thinking, "I'm always supposed to put my coat on when I go out, but this will only take a minute. I won't bother."

Age 13 and over His judgment and values are more or less permanently established.

PRIVATE PROPERTY

Ages 2–4 Yours and *Mine* are defined subjectively. When two children are playing "Yours" means "what I don't want." "Mine" means a. what you took, b. what I want, or c. what I want to keep.

Age 4 Children understand the difference between mine and yours.

Ages 5–6 They understand that they are not supposed to take what is yours without permission; they still do it, but they make it look legal. When a child brings a strange toy home from school and you ask whose toy it is, he will say, "Sammy gave it to me," or "Sammy said I could borrow it," even if he took it from Sammy.

Age 6 and on You can believe the explanations he gives if you have found he is generally truthful. He now understands the difference between true and false.

UNDERSTANDING

Ages 2–4 The child's ability to conceptualize is very primitive. He can see things only as they relate to him. He can understand objects in only one dimension. For example, if he hears his father call his grandmother "Mother," he might say, "She's not mother. She's grandmother."

If there are two red balls on the floor and you ask him to bring you the *bigger* red ball he will bring you the first ball he touches. He cannot think of big and red together, even though he knows what bigger means in a specific situation: "I am bigger than the baby." "This is the bigger stone."

His conception of quantity and volume is naïve. If his brother has two pieces of candy and he has one, he'll come sobbing, "Jimmy has more than I do." But if you break his piece in two and say, "Now you have two, too," he'll be satisfied.

Ages 4–5 He is very literal. The world is all separate wholes. Things are what they are called. If you ask, "Why is a chair called a chair?" he'll say, "Because it is a chair." If someone calls a four- or five-year-old STUPID he becomes stupid. If someone calls him FAT, he becomes fat. You may be able to console him and convince him that he really is smart and thin, but faced with the name caller, he again becomes fat and stupid.

Ages 7–8 Reality begins to exist for him independently. He can recognize and dislike teasing without accepting the specific content: you're stupid, you're fat.

Ages 8–13 He gradually develops a mature conception of himself and the world he lives in.

TIME CONCEPTS

Age 0–2 Now is now, and any time in the future is eternity. If you tell a two-year-old he can get up in a few minutes he will ask you at least ten times a minute, "Is it time now?"

Ages 2–3 Children begin to understand tomorrow and yesterday. They can wait ten minutes for you to finish what you are doing before you read the book they want to hear. They know that if you go out and say you will be back before lunch you will not be gone forever.

Age 7 and on They have a clearer and clearer idea of exactly what a minute, an hour, a day, and a week are—not only factually, but in terms of how long each one takes; what can be accomplished in each case, etc. They can even begin to understand what a year is.

CAUSE AND EFFECT

Ages 0–2 Has no idea of cause and effect at all. If you say, "Don't put the glass near the edge of the table. You might hit it and it will fall over," he won't understand. He will look at you wonderingly. He may even try hitting it to see what will happen. If you don't want the glass to spill or break you have to give a simple command. "Put your glass here." And show him where.

Ages 2–7 The child begins to understand that things make other things happen. He still does not really grasp the connection between abstract phenomenon. For example, if you see he has forty per cent on a spelling test and say, "See, Joe, I told you, if you don't study, you don't learn," he won't be led to study. He'll study if he likes to. If he doesn't like to, he won't. If you want him to memorize his spelling words, you'd better go over them together.

Ages 7–12 He is developing understanding of the effects of his own acts and omissions. He can study to get results to please you or his teacher, even if he does not like to study. Eventually he can study to get results, even when he does not want to and does not need to please you, because he needs the marks to be admitted to the school that offers the training he wants.

Q. Do you find that there are certain ages when children are particularly trouble-prone, because of fairly common situations they run into in our schools and social settings?

A. I think there are many children who are thrown by going to junior high school—particularly when it means going from a fairly small intimate school to a big impersonal one where they have to cope with many teachers each day, move around a big building from classroom to classroom every hour or so, and suddenly have almost total responsibility for getting their work done.

I think parents can anticipate the effect of such a change on children, particularly on those who are young for the grade they enter in the big school, and those who are less quick to adjust, cope, assert themselves, recognize their problem, and ask for help.

If the grade schools do not prepare children gradually for the changes they will meet in junior high school, parents can help by 1. giving them increasing responsibilities and independence at home; 2. discussing what the differences in schedules, routine, and responsibility will be in junior high school, and how to cope with them.

If children flounder at first, parents might try to offer them more help than they would otherwise consider necessary for twelve- and thirteen-year-olds. Your natural reaction is to say, "Stop acting like a baby," or "You're too old to behave like that." Actually children usually revert to more childish behavior under strain. They recover most quickly and easily if you "baby" them temporarily. It seems to give them the steadying hand they need to recover their equilibrium and regain their self-assurance.

Q. Do you think most children should be able to get along in any school?

A. School programs and curricula are developed to suit the average child. However, children are not all average. There are some children who definitely do better in certain kinds of schools and if I could find such a school for such a child I would try to send him to it. For example, a child who does not adapt easily to new experiences; a child who is easily distracted; a child who does best when routines repeat themselves day after day— will not do well in an open-classroom setting where children are encouraged to be independent, pursue their own interests, and more or less follow their own time schedule.

On the other hand, children who flourish on independence and become deeply involved in a subject they are interested in, pursuing it under their own steam, develop more ability, interest, depth of knowledge, and talent in free schools. Schools that expect every child to do the same thing at the same time, where originality and pursuit of individual interest are criticized, tend to squelch children's initiative.

Q. I think you can get a pretty good idea of what a school will be like from sizing up the principal. Do you agree?

A. Yes I do. I have found that a principal who is enthusiastic about his school, hopeful about his students, and articulate about the ways he and his staff have developed to help children succeed in school usually has an effective, dedicated staff. He attracts them because all good teachers like to be members of an effective team. If you share his point of view and think his school will suit your child, you will probably not be disappointed.

Q. My third-grader has become a very reluctant, in fact, miserable scholar this year. She complains that her teacher tells her to sit down whenever she tries to say anything; and constantly tells her she has not learned what's in the book. The child has been adventurous, curious, imaginative, and thoughtful up to now. I hate to see her lose interest in being an active participant in the learning process.

A. Phone for an appointment with her teacher. Talking with her should tell you whether your daughter is being more disruptive than contributing, i.e. whether the problem you see developing is hers or the teacher's. If you decide your child is being disruptive, support the teacher's efforts to encourage better classroom behavior by letting her know that you expect her to listen, follow instructions, and observe the teacher's class rules. If you decide she really is being squelched for being interested, see if she can be changed to a class where the teacher is more receptive to individuality in children's learning style, and her enthusiasm will again be welcomed and encouraged.

Q. I understand from what you say about children's dependence on adult approval in their early years that you feel it is unwise to be critical of small children's performance. How do they learn your standards, values, and goals?

A. I did not mean to suggest that parents should approve whatever a small child does. There are times, obviously, when children have to be stopped quite forcibly from doing something dangerous to them, destructive of their own or your things, unkind to other children or animals. However, while you would of course prevent your child from hitting another child with a block at the age of two or three, it would be foolish and cruel to call him a bully or lecture him about his disposition at that age. Children gradually learn your standards before they understand them from what you let them do and from your approval or disapproval of their behavior. Your explanations and disciplinary measures enforce your values, too, but they should be suited to the child's age and level of understanding.

Q. At my last teacher conference, the teacher said our ten-year-old daughter was not following instructions. I couldn't understand because she seems perfectly attentive, agreeable, and accurate about what she is told to do at home. She is in an unusually quick and articulate group of kids.

A. Perhaps you are pointing to the answer yourself. If she is less assertive, and tends to learn in a more methodical way than they do, she may simply be letting them do the reciting and quietly going her way. If she is learning—judging from tests and private conversations with her teacher—I wouldn't worry. If she is falling behind, I would try to get the teacher to consider her diffident manner, recognize the difference in her approach to new material, and see if she can't find ways to encourage more participation from your daughter.

I remember a similar situation where an older child appeared very passive, almost retarded—mostly because she didn't respond to requests and suggestions from parents. The child was seven. One day she asked her mother to show her how to sew on buttons, and learned in no time. We figured out that she had given up trying to race her little sister to carry out every parental request. The younger child was naturally quicker and motivated by the typical need to keep up with the older one. When the parents began to give the older child assignments suited to her greater ability, that only she could fulfill, she began to do them eagerly and well.

Q. If children learn in orderly sequence and each advance in understanding depends on the underlying foundation of knowledge, experience, and understanding assimilated earlier, what happens when children miss a step? Does it, for example, interfere with orderly academic progress if a child fails to understand the basic principles of numbers in the early grades? Could this make them poor math students forever?

A. Most learning gaps can be filled if the missing step is properly identified, and the essential teaching does not make the child feel stupid in his own eyes, and more particularly, in the eyes of his friends. In a private situation the child can concentrate on lessons and not on whether he is making a fool of himself.

Can a child learn algebra without ever having understood or mastered basic arithmetic? I am not sure. It is inconceivable that a child would not pick up the basic concepts of addition, subtraction, division, and multiplication from daily life, even when he did not appear to be grasping and using them correctly in the classroom. It seems to me that a child who really wanted to learn algebra in ninth grade could do so if he was willing to submit to the necessary formal arithmetic drill and practice that he missed earlier. The trouble is that most children who don't do well in arithmetic never develop any interest, and therefore are unwilling to do the drill-work that would make high school math comprehensible.

There are some things, however, which must be mastered at a crucial period, or not at all. Learning rules of behavior—from which conscience and morality develop —depends on the stability of early care, and the strength of the baby-caretaker relationship.

The young child learns to give back the toy, for example, because he is made to. Later, even if no one is looking, he does not take another child's toy, because he wants the approval of the adults he loves. Eventually, their rules, standards, values, and beliefs become the unconscious reference for his own judgment of how to behave. He acts without even thinking, directly, about what would please them. If some disturbance in the parent-child relationship interferes with the completion of this last step in development of conscience, the child grows up, generally, abnormal. If he does the right thing, he does it because he has to, or because he is afraid of being caught. He has no integrated values of his own.

FIRST READERS

Much of parents' concern about reading is a legacy from the "look-say," "they'll-read-when-they're-ready" era that made problems for many of them when they were learning to read. The teaching of reading has come a long, long way. Look-say, per se, is passé!

Responsible reading teachers and reading specialists today don't wait for kids to read. They're busy, even in prekindergarten, getting three's and four's ready. They're methodically starting them off to read and write in first grade. And, in good elementary schools—of which there are a lot more than the negative picture of public education usually projected would lead you to expect—teachers are doing something promptly about children who don't show early signs of getting it together. They are taking responsibility for finding the right way to teach each child. "They'll-learn-when-they're-ready" has given way to "leave-no-child-unlearned."

This does not mean that each kindergartner will know all his alphabet sounds, or that every first-grader is going to read words and books by the end of September, or even by the end of May. It is a recognition that, while children will not all read at the same time in the same way, they will—with few exceptions—start reading in first grade if they are properly taught.

Recently a co-operative school mother told me earnestly that the parents in her first-grader's class had decided that their children would learn to read that year —or else!

"We want them to find out that you have to do things even if they are hard."

I could almost see those children's fathers and mothers rolling up their sleeves to force reading down those six-year-olds' throats. I hope the parents aren't quite as militant as they sound. Today's skilled and experienced teachers have totally rejected letting children move from nursery school almost to high school, expressing themselves orally, through block building, drama, art, music, or shop, when they do not opt to read and write. But they have *not* rejected the underlying philosophy of progressive education, which holds that children learn best when their teachers work *with* them rather than *on* them.

The issue is not permissiveness *versus* authoritarianism. Good teachers don't let the child drift. Rather they watch him carefully to assess his abilities, mental and temperamental, his level of development, and his interests.

This enables them to find out how and what to teach him so that he begins to learn and wants to learn. Then as he discovers the satisfaction of success he is ready to begin to assume responsibility for learning on his own.

Today's fine teachers don't push or pull. They lead children along as education is meant to do.

Behind the evolution in the teaching of reading is an ever-expanding store of knowledge about how children learn. One of the by-products has been an explosion of educational hardware. The temptation of schools to go overboard on gadgetry under the blandishments of the steady stream of "education" salesmen that pursue them is great. For example, many school systems today rue the supplies of broken-down twenty-thousand-dollar talking typewriters touted a few years back as the latest most effective weapon in the war against juvenile illiteracy. They just didn't stand up.

Teachers are without doubt better trained than they were even ten years ago to spot and circumvent the little and big differences in children that could frustrate their first efforts to read. They have an infinitely richer and more individualized battery of reading systems and materials to implement their teaching. Nevertheless, the *best teacher* is still the *best teacher*—materials or not. And the best teacher is a perceptive, interested human being who really likes little children as friends—seeing their differences—almost liking them *for* their differences, and appreciating the wonderful candor and freshness of their opinions and tastes, enthusiasms, dislikes and affections —the sharp definition of their young personalities.

In Sheffield, Massachusetts, Mrs. Georgianna O'Connell, an elementary school curriculum specialist and an experienced first grade teacher, told me about a study undertaken to sift the qualities in teachers that seem to work best with children. Teachers in a number of schools were divided as follows:

1. Inexperienced, minimally trained, enthusiastic about children and teaching. One of them, for example, began the school year by saying, "I don't know much about science, but I'll try to keep one page ahead. We're going to find out about all this together."

2. Well-qualified, professionally committed teachers.

3. Well-trained teachers, well qualified in their subject, doing a professional job.

Not surprising to me, the first group were the winners.

Basic care for children and concern for their success are more important than any other quality in teaching, particularly at the elementary level when children are so dependent on the approval and support of adults.

A really good teacher could probably teach reading from candy wrappers or magazine advertisements. I saw it happen, almost, with a group of six, five- to seven-year-olds, at the Berkshire Country Day School in Stockbridge, Massachusetts.

It was the first reading lesson for the year on the second day of school. The minute the teacher passed out the books the kids in this ungraded class—all reading on the same level—began to smile, leaf through the pages, and chatter to each other about the characters and the story.

The teacher started the lesson by asking them to tell their visitor (me) about the story. When they were thoroughly warmed up and had, incidentally, reviewed all the story's important words in the telling, she asked who'd like to read for me. No coaxing was needed. One after another the children asked to read a page—the fast and fluent and expressive as eagerly as the halting. They were totally involved in the story. Not one child hurried another, corrected or commented on another's performance. They treated each other with the same respect they enjoyed from their teacher.

A child who had been among the most talkative was the only one who had real trouble picking out the words. Even so, no one got impatient. His teacher didn't rush in to help. Occasionally she asked him to give her the initial sound of the word that seemed to stump him and that helped. When he got through three of his four sentences he looked at her hopefully. She smiled.

"You've remembered a tremendous amount over the

summer. I think that's enough for today, don't you?" He looked a little disappointed. "Or would you like to read the next sentence," she went on. "You don't have to you know."

"I'll try," he said matter of factly, and slowly but surely finished the page.

She didn't make too much fuss. She said, "That's fine," and once more engaged the entire group in discussion. They talked tenderly about the primer's farmer hero, whom they decided they liked most of all for his kindness. This led them to talk about what kindness is; how the farmer showed it in his treatment of his animals and how animals showed their appreciation by working hard for him. They seemed as close to the farmer as if they were old friends. Their comments about all the characters were full of perception, humor, and fun. The lesson covered word recognition, phonics, comprehension, ideas about feelings and values, what sentences are, and even the use of capitals and periods.

The teachers confess a little shamefacedly that this first reader is a bit corny for jet-age children. But when it comes to signing the new book orders each spring, no one can bear to give it up.

Because it is kind of old fashioned, with a whole cast of fully drawn characters that children immediately identify with, it may be the very best kind of a book to introduce children to the pleasure of learning to read. At least it seemed that way from the class I watched: a beautiful demonstration of how to make children want to read and how to teach them.

The teacher assumed they would learn. They did, so confidently that you knew it had never occurred to any of them that they might have problems. They weren't in any hurry. They worked as if they enjoyed working.

They had already, it seemed, found the pleasure and value of reading, and looked as if they would never stop.

There are almost as many theories about how children learn to read as there are letters in the alphabet, but I think it is more useful to talk about what makes for success than debate which theory is best.

Children need to

1. Want to read.

2. Be properly prepared in terms of their visual and verbal knowledge of the world around them and

3. be properly taught.

Parents can be important helpers from the very beginning. In the preschool years, when they are almost the only teachers around, they are indispensable. As we said earlier, parents begin teaching spontaneously, as soon as a child is born. Under normal circumstances they teach children to recognize objects and sounds, and give them names; distinguish differences in size, shape, and color; understand order; recognize themselves as separate human beings; and—in gradually more sophisticated fashion—put what they see, hear, feel, understand, and learn into words.

In the first years, children get a basic foundation in language. After that what parents do contributes a great deal to their readiness for reading at five or six. You stimulate their interest in learning to read, and teach them what the printed word is all about.

All experience children get sharpens their senses, their perceptions, and their powers of observation. The wider their experience, the richer their vocabulary and the corresponding inventory of images in their young brains, the easier it will be for them to recognize and remember words in print. The child who can understand and picture words he is learning to read has a head start over the child with limited experience, vocabulary, and understanding.

Experience does not have to begin with a capital *E*. Children can learn as much from watching an ant go about his daily chores in the dirt around your front door, or playing with the pots and pans and jar tops at your feet on the kitchen floor, as they can from day-long excursions to the zoo. They can learn as much from talking to you about the pictures in one of your magazines as they can from a museum visit.

The experiences they share with you do not have to be unique, or important, or educational, or approved by Drs. X, Y, Z, or Teachers College. The important thing is for them to be interesting. If you and your child are both enjoying them, they will stimulate conversation and exchange of ideas; stretch his vocabulary and imagination; teach him to relate pictures and words; associate talking with reading, the spoken with the printed word.

Parents tend to try to give children experiences they think they *ought* to have instead of introducing them to things they themselves like.

Take your cues from your children's interests, too. If you thought he'd love puppet shows and find he hates them, forget puppet shows for a while. Don't push. Like good teachers in an open classroom, be there to teach, offer ideas, guide and help when needed. But let the children make some choices about what they want to do with you.

Some parents are so eager to see their children learn that they seem to be teaching them most of the time they are with them. This is fine when it's mutually enjoyable. However, if it seems to put a strain on the child, ease up. You don't want a preschooler to get the idea that learning is something dull and hard. It may be fine for an eight- or ten-year-old to find out that there is a certain amount of drill and difficult concentration involved in reaching the goals he has set for himself. But learning should not be made hard for beginners. Learning is so natural to them that it is not hard to find tasks that are interesting and easy to master so that their confidence keeps growing from accomplishment to accomplishment.

The list of activities that help children learn to read are endless. Among them are card games, picture card games, lotto and memory; shopping trips; looking at mail order catalogues; watching parents working and asking questions; talking, talking, talking all through the day, wherever you are together, about what you are doing, what you are seeing, and what it all means; telling stories, singing songs, watching television and talking about it, during and after; listening to records and so on.

There is unanimous agreement among reading specialists that children from "reading" homes read more easily and quickly than those whose parents neither read nor read to them. Probably this is partly because children imitate parents. But there is more to it, I am sure, than seeing parents buried in books or newspapers all the time, and wanting to be like them.

Reading parents, for one thing, are usually talking parents. They tend to discuss, reason, and tell and show children, spontaneously. Thus, more learning goes on as a matter of course in reading families than among nonreaders. When TV is the main source of information and entertainment at home, it leaves little time for family chat. Viewers tend to view in silence, rather than look and discuss.

Reading parents also start reading to children at a very early age. They show their children books before they can talk—books without words, but with pictures of objects in strong primary colors that catch their babies' attention: the teddy bear, the baby, the cat, the dog, the cow, the horse. While Mommy or Daddy holds him and talks about the pictures, the baby begins to get the idea of what books are about.

Next, from the timeless Mother Goose rhymes and their sense and nonsense tales of losing and finding, punishment and reward, their sagas of the everyday joys and sorrows of family life, children get their first notion of what stories are—with beginning, middle, and end.

A little later they learn to laugh, sympathize, suffer, and rejoice with the human and animal heroes of the picture books you read. Inexperienced and very new to their emotions, they identify instantly with Peter Rabbit, who doesn't mind his mother, and *almost* gets caught by the big farmer; with the duckling family for whom all the traffic on Boston Common must stop; with Mike Mulligan and his outmoded old steam shovel, which triumphantly does the job no other steam shovel could; with the boy who masters his fears and gets past the bears on the mountain and successfully completes the errand on which his mother had sent him.

Secure and close to you as you read, they can taste danger, hope for the best, but fear the worst, enjoy the relief of their heroes' eventual triumph. From good, simple picture stories, they discover, for the first time, the power of literature to expand and deepen their own experience and the pleasure that this gives.

Their picture books also teach them that being able

to read is a way to satisfy their insatiable curiosity
about almost everything in the world and how it works.
I have seen three-year-olds poring over simple picture
encyclopedias for a very long time. Little children love
to look at books that tell them about schools, hospitals,
buses, mail delivery, plumbing, butterflies, tunnels,
dinosaurs, modern and ancient ships, and an incon-
ceivably long list of other natural and man-made phe-
nomena.

Children seem to learn from reading parents just by
watching them do it. So-called natural readers who
know how to read the first time they see a school book
have no magical powers. They have discovered the connection between print and words by watching parents
read to them.

Dale Bryant, a professor of psychology and reading
at Teachers College in New York, told me about a child
on the first day of school who very confidently opened
his book when he got it and turned it upside down. His
teacher was about to diagnose a serious reading disability, but decided to see first whether the child knew
anything about letters and sounds. During a quiet moment when the class was busy she sat down quietly with
him and began to talk about letters and words. He
nodded knowingly and said, "I can read." Whereupon
he read off page after page from the upside-down book.

Far from having a learning problem, he was remarkably capable. He had taught himself to read by watching his father and mother. They always read to him
before he went to sleep, sitting opposite him on the bed,
so he had learned to read upside down.

If you do read to your children, this anecdote suggests, they'll get more out of it if you let them see what
you are reading right side up. It will not only give them

a better idea of the way words and letters go—from left to right, one line after another from top down, but it is cozier. Instead of sitting on a separate chair, or on the end of the bed, sit beside your child and let him snuggle against you, following page and picture as you read. When he gets to be four and five you may even follow the words, now and then, with your finger. (Don't make a chore of it!) It will give him an idea of how words look and how reading goes.

Another good idea is to stop now and then and talk about what you are reading. If you're reading a suspense story, stop and guess, together, what will happen next. If you are reading about something the child is familiar with—the cat who lost his mittens, for example—ask how it happened; how he can keep from losing them again.

Just talk about the pictures and what they tell. Ask him what different words mean. Needless to say, don't try to test your preschooler. Do it just for fun and to make the story more fun for him. Never test, drill, or criticize.

If you want your child to grow with the book habit a good idea is to take him with you when you go to the library.

Let him choose books from the children's shelves just as you choose yours. You can afford to let him make mistakes. If he picks dull, badly illustrated, inappropriate books, he'll learn better. You can always take one or two sure winners for him so that the trip won't be a loss.

If you are accustomed to buying books for yourself, make a habit of buying one for your child, too, whenever you visit a bookshop. One of the best things that has happened in juvenile publishing in recent years is the reissue, in paperback, of children's twentieth-century classics with the original illustrations. If you don't know how to pick good ones, watch your child's taste. The kinds of books he asks to have read over and over should be a clue.

What other experiences prepare children for reading? Some educators believe that a number of physical skills help. They are convinced that good physical co-ordination—as demonstrated by balance, climbing, crawling, running, bicycle and wagon operation, swing pumping, throwing, catching, games like dodge ball, and clear fluent talking—all correlate with early, easy reading.

Other educators say there is no proof of such a correlation at all. However, self-confidence helps anyone at any age meet any new challenge. The more skills a child possesses the more confident he will be. Skills help him hold his own with peers and with adults. If you can help a child become better co-ordinated, more agile, more adept at the usual playground and social skills without making a job of it, fine. If your efforts produce more suffering than success, give up. Remember, children are not all gifted with the same physical and mental abilities. They cannot all be best, no matter how you and they try.

As Dr. George Lane, the superintendent of schools in the Berkshire Hills school district in Massachusetts, said: "You can't preach that each child is an individual and then treat them as if they all had an IQ of 160."

A skinny, clumsy, nearsighted child who hates the sight of a ball of any kind might take longer to read than the champion slugger in first grade. Then again he might not. However, he would be permanently inhibited in all learning efforts if he were forced into the repeated failures that would follow an enforced program of physical fitness.

After School Starts

What should a parent's role be after a child starts school?

One group of educators says KEEP OUT! They believe that learning to read is a tremendous step toward independence. When children do it on their own their success is a big boost to their self-esteem, which, in turn, provides the incentive for future efforts in learning.

This group tends to view parents as not too friendly ogres, breathing down their children's necks every night, undoing all the work teachers have done by day. Of course, parental anxiety, misinformation, and ignorance can have disastrous effects on children's progress in reading as in anything else. But teachers are as guilty of these shortcomings as parents. In fact, it may be that some of the animosity educators express toward parents' intrusion into the schools stems from fear of being looked at, questioned, checked up, criticized, and even forced to change, themselves.

For what it is worth, I found that schools where reading levels and children's interest were highest are the ones that try to make parents partners in the teaching process.

I am committed to this point of view. I think it is extremely important for parents to know and understand how their children are being taught. I think we need the involvement of parents in order to make the schools function well. I think informed, serious parents are the best possible judges of whether a school works for their children. The schools are *parents'* schools, not *teachers'*. Parents should remember this and assume the responsibility it implies not only for their own children but for the education of all the children in the community. When they do, there will be better teaching, more mutual respect and support between parents and teachers, and better service to the children, from all quarters.

I am going to describe, briefly, what I consider an ideal program for involving parents in a joint parent-teacher effort to educate children. It begins, in Stockbridge, Massachusetts, before the first grade. Here school officials are more concerned about parents who don't take part than fearful of those who do.

Whether parents become a nuisance to teachers and a burden to their children depends a great deal on the school's attitude toward them. Superintendent Lane believes that parents get anxious and make their children nervous because they don't know what they should do or what kind of progress to expect from their first-graders. Therefore, the Berkshire Hills schools try to demythicize the educational process by teaching parents what they are trying to do, and how they do it, and giving them specific ways to help at home and at school.

A description of the program will give you some idea of the kinds of things you should be able to find out about your child and his progress from teachers and what you might be able to do to help him.

Screening. Parents of prospective first-graders bring their children to school in the spring for a morning of fun and games. The session allows evaluation of each child's physical, social, and intellectual functioning. It includes hearing, vision, and speech tests. Parents are asked not to prep their kids for the event. They are told that the purpose is not to measure IQ's, but to find out where children are in order to help them get ready to start first grade in the best possible shape.

Parents and older school children volunteer to help teachers with the screening. This makes the atmosphere easy and minimizes tension. After the first two experimental years the spring screening is already an event that kindergartners look forward to.

At the end of the screening parents are briefed and specific prescriptions for further vision or hearing or psychological testing are given when necessary. Parents may also be given homework assignments to carry out with their children during the summer. These range from playing catch now and then, to engaging the child in guessing games or storytelling that gives him practice (without his knowing it) pronouncing letters he has trouble with; or learning to be more alert to differences in size, shape, color, or detail.

Like other educators, Dr. Lane is not totally convinced that children who run, jump, climb, talk, and use their hands more skillfully than others necessarily read faster.

He is sure, however, that anything that brings parents together with children in play (which is what the summer work is meant to be) is all to the good. Children need the concentrated focus on them as individuals that these summer assignments create. In today's busy homes they get very little of it. They also gain self-confidence as they improve their physical skills. They become eager, rather than apprehensive about learning.

Most important, the whole screening process successfully conveys the message that the schools want parents to help them give their children the best education they can.

Workshops. Class workshops take place early in the

school year. Parents come to school and teachers explain to them what they are teaching and how they teach.

Through workshops and conferences parents learn before first grade is over, that

1. Teachers try to teach each child as an individual, recognizing and respecting his individual abilities and nature.

2. Speed is not important. Learning comfortably at his own rate without pressure to compete will make the child most successful in the long run.

3. Comparing a child's progress with what his classmates do will not help him learn easily. The schools do not mark elementary school children.

4. Report cards are used to evaluate each child's progress in relation to his abilities and effort. The teacher points out where the child is strong and suggests where he needs to improve.

5. The teacher lets parents know when she is concerned about a child. She asks parents to let her know when *they* have questions or worries.

6. Children learn in small reading groups of three or four children of similar ability. This helps keep them from getting discouraged if they aren't as "good," or as "fast" as other children in the class. Groups, however, are fluid so that children can move from one to another according to their progress. Teachers expect progress from all children, regardless of where they are at the moment.

7. There are workshop sessions each fall to show parents what each grade is doing, but parents are welcome any time. They don't have to call for an appointment. The school feels parents' attendance at workshops is very important. If they know what their children are

learning and how they are being taught it is easier for them to help when children ask.

8. Teachers arrange individual conferences with parents early in the year. They believe in the positive value of talking about children when they are getting along well instead of waiting for a crisis, when discussions often lead to misunderstandings.

How well the program works in practice varies, as these things always do, with the interest and skill of both teacher and parents.

How can you take the initiative and find out what goes on in your child's class and how to help at home, when your school does not invite your participation?

Make an appointment to visit the school. Most public schools are open to any parent, any time, by law. It is politic, of course, to make an appointment first, and saves your arriving just as the class is leaving for its annual trip to the firehouse.

If you are discouraged from visiting, find out why. These days, schools throughout the country are generally open to parents. In the suburban and rural systems I visited, parents appear to wander in and out constantly, with complete ease and informality on everyone's part.

During your visit the teacher may not have time to answer your questions. Obviously you would not want to disrupt her classwork. See if you can arrange to meet her during a free period or after school.

Once you understand how the class is doing, you can judge for yourself how well your own child is progressing from month to month. A teacher's guidance will make it easier for you to help him. Don't help unless you are asked to, either by him or by his teacher. Most teachers like to have first-graders get a firm start before they try to read at home. Don't press your child to read to you. Let him offer, first. Most teachers let children take home their preprimers as they read them. Children usually love to read to their parents, when they are able. If your child does offer, be appreciative. Do not correct or insist on his sounding out words he can't read, or make disparaging remarks: "I thought you had read this book," for example, or "You don't know some of these words at all."

Try to be cheery. Say something like, "I'm proud of you for reading to me." "You certainly have made a good start." "You are really trying hard, aren't you?"

If you have any fears, keep them to yourself and consult the teacher later for facts and guidance. Quite possibly you simply expect too much, too soon.

There are some grounds for the fairly widespread teacher fear of parents. Teachers have seen many children damaged by overanxious parents' efforts to "help."

The best help you can give is to make the reading scene at home a close and happy one that children look forward to. This is not hard if you are not worried about how fast your child is progressing, compared with his classmates.

Concentrate on the help that is requested. Try to respond just as you would if your child asked for a Band-Aid, or wanted you to look at his sore toe, or open the door when he has his arms full. Apply the most effective help in the easiest, fastest way.

When a child says, "What's this word?" tell him. Don't get into—"Haven't you learned that?" "Can't you sound it out?"

If he misses it again, supply it again. Don't yield to the temptation to say, "I just told you."

If you would like to go further in helping than having your child read to you when he feels like it, ask his teacher what you can do. Specific assignments will focus attention on definite, simple drills and keep you from worrying about *all* your child's shortcomings, real or imagined.

The most common problems beginning readers have are: 1. making mistakes in distinguishing between words that look somewhat alike; and 2. forgetting what they have just learned before the words have become part of their working reading vocabulary.

Children learn to read in two ways: by sight—that is by recognizing a whole word at once; and by the phonic method—by sounding words out, syllable by syllable. The second way is as important as the first. There are just too many long words for anyone ever to learn them all by sight.

Here is where the child's background of experience helps him. If the words he sees and hears mean something to him right away, they evoke pictures in his mind's eye. If he understands what he hears, he can see it as he reads it and that helps him remember. If, on the other hand, the words he hears are unfamiliar to him, it is harder for him to recognize them the next time he sees them. However, whether children understand the words they are supposed to be learning, or not, some have quicker memories than others.

Teachers can recognize the kind of extra practice that will help each child. If the child has trouble telling similar words apart, the teacher might give you a list of four or five words he needs practice on each night. Let's take—for illustration—postal. Pick several words, real or made-up, that look like it. Make a kind of flash card for each word plus the right word. For example, *postal,* portal, dostal, bortal, pastal. Go through the cards more and more quickly until he can pick the right word—*postal* —immediately. Do not have him read the other words out loud. Teach him only to recognize and say the right one.

If your child's hang-up is memory, make flash cards for the four or five words the teacher asks you to drill him on. To train memory, go over the words two or three times—after school, at dinner, before bed—in five-minute drills. Memory is tricky. Studies show that children lose a great part of what they learn soon after they seem to have learned it. Repeated brief reviews after the lesson, spaced at intervals throughout the day, help children retain what they learn.

Teachers and parents have an almost infallible habit of trying to accomplish too much at once. As a result they often accomplish less than they might have by suiting the lesson to the child. Follow these hard and fast rules. Keep lessons pleasant and burden free. Make the experience positive, not negative. Don't let work interfere with a child's right to play, rest, do nothing, go to sleep.

Lessons should never last more than fifteen minutes for children in the first grades. Some children can't last that long. They do better if you start with very short sessions—even though they seem to accomplish nothing —gradually lengthening the work period. You may find progress will start suddenly after a seemingly endless period of stagnation.

At this age, more than ever, children benefit from being read to. At six and seven they can enjoy books you will enjoy, too. You can pick adventure and animal stories, tales of fantasy and imagination, mystery yarns and spy thrillers that go on and on, stimulating conversation, discussion, guesses, and anticipation. I remember Freddy, a silly, funny, wise, wonderful, ingenious pig, who, through an endless series, was everything from a detective to a cowboy, with hilarious, suspenseful adventures, which he always survived.

Six and seven are the peak years for addiction to jokes and riddles. When my children were little, alarm clock jokes were favorites. Now, I understand, the fad is *grape* jokes. Sometimes children will practically teach themselves to read from anthologies of jokes or riddles in their eagerness to outdo their friends.

When children have trouble in school the real problem may be somewhere else. It distracts them from learning. A child's best friend may have moved away. The baby brother may be suddenly getting a lot of attention from Daddy. Mother may have gone back to work.

Just as grown people get support and relief from hearing how other people solve problems like theirs, reading about other children who have survived the experience they are suffering often helps young children feel better and move on again.

In conclusion, most children read without any trouble, when they are adequately taught. About fifteen per cent will have some difficulty. Of this small group, most will survive and progress with minor help from teachers and parents. Often time alone does the trick. Some children simply mature much more slowly than others. Many schools advise parents to let children who are young for their age wait a year to start first grade. In the long run they progress much faster because they are comfortable and happy rather than strained and fearful when they start. Schools with ungraded first classes don't have to worry about differences in children's maturity levels. They can group children according to their performance much more simply than in graded classes.

Individualized learning systems are helping make it easy for children to progress at their own pace, too. They allow each child to proceed as fast as he comfortably can. The children can correct their own work and review what they learn with their individualized materials, with only supervisory help from teachers, and, of course, daily group reading sessions.

It is exciting to see how diligently and responsibly young children work on these programs. It proves, at least to my satisfaction, that when parents and teachers expect children to succeed, and work with them, one to one, from the start, they do learn, happily. In the atmosphere of trust, which a strong teacher-parent relationship creates, parent and teacher, together, help the child get a good start in reading.

CHAPTER SEVEN

Q & A

Q. I have read that the look-say method delays reading and creates reading problems. Is this true?

A. Children have to begin to read by learning to recognize some words at sight. They learn "a", "the", "some", common verbs, and fifty to one hundred forty-five words for familiar objects this way, before they go on to phonic reading. The look-say method attempts to help children learn to sight-read by giving them pictures to jog their memories for certain words. The danger lies in carrying this method too far. If look-say remains the principal method of teaching in the early learning period, some children learn to guess at words from pictures, rather than recognize the words themselves. They don't learn to *read* them. When you are helping children learn words, concentrate on the words; don't encourage them to guess the words from the pictures.

Q. In my child's kindergarten class they play lots of games in which children learn to tell the difference between big and bigger, round and square, and so on. The teacher says these games prepare them to read. How?

A. There is a theory that children who are alert to differences in size, shape, direction, etc., transfer this ability to reading. They are supposed to be able to distinguish letters and words from one another more quickly than children who have not had such training. I think early practice in exercising all their perceptive faculties helps children become alert and interested in discriminating. It may also stimulate their interest and curiosity about the world around them—which also makes them more interested in reading. However, I agree with Dr. Dale Bryant of Teachers College that the way to teach children to tell letters and words from each other is by concentrating on letters and words. Then, when they are successful, they have the satisfaction of knowing they can read.

I do not believe that picking out the odd face in a row of like faces or choosing the odd pumpkin in a row of matching ones will help many first- or second-graders who are having trouble with letters and words. The tasks are too dull to attract and hold their interest. Besides, there is no guarantee that succeeding at them will teach them to distinguish letters and words.

The point I am making was illustrated very well in a cartoon some years back, showing a cluster of children in a playground discussing space and rocketry. The teacher is ringing the bell for class. One kid says, "C'mon,

I guess we have to go back and string those goddam beads."

Q. A few years ago a lot of educators worried about children who got tracked for life by their first grade performance. Does that still happen?

A. I'm afraid it does. In spite of all we know about individual differences in development and how differences affect the speed and manner in which children learn, many schools look at results on tests administered en masse, in routine fashion, and group children according to performance. Children get labeled, sometimes permanently, in spite of their abilities. Teachers use low scores, even though they may mean little, as an excuse to forget the nonlearning, instead of finding the way to teach them.

I would add that screening children may have the same result. While the purpose is to detect potential difficulties, however minor, so that they can be corrected or taken into account in teaching, test findings may also be used to justify failure when kids don't learn.

Q. I have heard some incredible stories about parents who have spent fortunes on reading laboratories and reading experts who promise to correct nonreading in a given period but actually accomplish nothing more than making kids anxious and afraid of their inadequacy in school. How can one avoid this trap?

A. There is no reason to seek outside help unless you are advised to do so by your child's teacher, with the support of the principal, and/or the psychologist or guidance teacher for the school system.

If there is disagreement over whether help is needed, the sensible course is to resolve your concern by getting expert advice. Ask the school where to go. If you don't trust the school, ask your pediatrician or consult the local or county medical society or mental health department. Such agencies are qualified to refer you to proper consultants for testing diagnosis and recommendations.

Q. Some schools tell you not to worry if children don't learn to read in first grade, or even second and third. Others say children should get a good start in first grade. They all say don't worry. I do worry, partly because the advice I get is so confusing. What is right?

A. I can't give a hard-and-fast answer to your question. What a child accomplishes in first grade depends on what he's learned before, how he is being taught, and naturally, how quickly he as an individual learns. Most of the educators I talk to, however, would agree that six- and seven-year-old, middle class children, who come to school with a normal background of experience, will ordinarily learn sounds of letters; have a sight vocabulary of basic words, and begin to read some unfamiliar words by the phonic method at the end of first grade. It is true that some less mature first-graders will not get this far. Pushing them won't help. It can make them rebellious or fearful. They are simply not ready. Good teachers know how to give them work that will make it easier for them to catch up when they are mature.

In schools where first-graders are not expected to read, only the so-called natural-born readers will learn in first grade. I wouldn't worry about this if the program is interesting enough to keep them busy, and they are acquiring skills and interests that will stimulate their interest in learning to read according to the school's method and timetable. There is no particular reason why children should learn to read in first grade, except that parents like to have them do so. When they do start in second grade they often make such fast progress that it evens out. What would worry me is seeing my first-grader in a nonstructured classroom where the teacher is so overwhelmed and inadequate that the children seem to be learning nothing except how to add to the confusion.

Q. We are both readers and have read to our daughter ever since she could look at pictures. She is having trouble learning to read. We thought she would learn right away. Why is it?

A. Reading parents do produce good readers, generally. However, a child who has enjoyed being read to may be surprised to find that it isn't as easy as it seemed. If he happens to be one who is slow at discriminating letters or sounds and needs lots of drill to get started, he may give up. He needs lots of individual attention and support at the beginning. Once he gets through the early problem phase he will speed ahead fast. I think it is specially important for such children, whose interests may be more sophisticated and broad than those of many of their classmates, to get help so that they learn to read early. Otherwise, poor reading skills may hold them up when they want to read for information and pleasure in the middle grades.

Q. Our eleven-year-old daughter always wants to do her homework and reading in the living room with us. I insist that my children work quietly in their own rooms, because I have always read that they learn to concentrate better when they are not distracted by competing bids for their attention.

A. In general, this is true. It does not help beginning

readers, or anyone, to become involved in reading, if they try to do their reading while watching TV, listening to a talk show, or their parents' discussing next summer's vacation plans.

However, some children work better with people around, just as some babies play better when they can watch their mothers near by—even if they don't demand their active attention.

Plan home life, if possible, so that homework or reading time coincides with everyone's reading or deskwork. Then the children can be part of the family circle without being distracted, and not feel exiled and unhappy in their rooms. Isolation for some children is more distracting than TV.

Some children are impervious to distraction of any kind. If you have one of these, you can let her work or read wherever she wants to.

Q. Our son goes to a school where no one worries about reading. They kept saying he would read when he wanted to. He still does not want to and he is in the fifth grade. Now he doesn't want to do anything—although he is intelligent and interested in learning when he can absorb information by talking and looking. He reads so poorly and slowly that he gets tired of concentrating before he can read enough to understand his assignments. How can we help before he gives up on schoolwork completely?

A. Consult your pediatrician about finding a psychiatrist or psychologist who can do the testing necessary to identify the problems that are interfering with learning; then follow his guidance about how to proceed. He may have a learning problem that requires a special kind of teaching. He may have failed to learn because he simply has not been taught. The aim, of course, would be to help him learn as fast as possible so that nonreading will no longer interfere with his social and academic adjustment. You will surely want to find another school if you are able to.

TRAPS FOR PARENTS

We Americans pride ourselves on our pioneering background. We worship enterprise, initiative, inventiveness, and derring-do—the heritage of our past. We believe all problems—human as well as mechanical—can be solved by applying the infinite resources of scientific knowledge and our talent for technology.

But we have another side—a fear of being different, of not making the team, figuratively speaking.

This paradox leads us into many traps as parents, which is what this chapter is all about. If you know what the traps are, you may be able to sidestep some of them, and extricate yourself from others in which you may be caught. Hopefully, too, once you learn to know a trap, you can warn teachers who may be falling in; or help them out, if they'll let you; or, if worse comes to worst, stop yourself from getting snared with them.

The Traps

1. THE NORMAL CHILD

Everyone wants a good normal average child—nothing special.

Normal equals all-American.

All-American likes apple, cherry, blueberry, in that order, and, in addition, is an A student without being a grind.

All-American has the right attitude, and gets A for effort, co-operation, leadership, and popularity—right from birth.

All-American is agreeable to everything, everyone, all the time, but all-American is no push-over.

Now, obviously, if that's your idea of average normal, lots of children just won't fit. Children are human beings and human beings are all different. If you think there is only one NORMAL, you are bound to be worried by most of your children a good deal of the time, almost from the day they are born.

Take, for instance:

THE DYNAMITE KID

Always on the go, full of energy, tireless, into things before you know it. The teacher says he is abnormal. He does not sit still. He is a PROBLEM!

His mother worries and tells Father. Father frowns. They see a psychiatrist. Happy, hoppy Johnny or Jill gets TREATED!

Happy, hoppy Johnny or Jill knows something is wrong with him/her; sees it in parents' eyes, teacher's eyes. Happy, hoppy Johnny or Jill *becomes* a problem just because he/she does not fit the unreal picture of what kids *should* be; because teaching him would require the teacher to acknowledge that her program and her teaching methods were not reaching him.

THE TORTOISE

Imperturbable Eddy plugs away persistently when everyone else in his class has apparently mastered whatever teacher is teaching. She goes on without him, but his puzzled look disturbs her. She tells Mother that Eddy is slow. Get a tutor. Get a test. Fix him up.

Eddy is not slow at all. Eddy is perfectly bright. He simply needs to take his time to absorb and assimilate new information. He has to understand it thoroughly and make it his own before he moves on to the next step. If teacher hasn't time to teach him and can't make time before or after class, she should ask parents to help instead of making them and him think he is stupid and unteachable.

SELF-CONTAINED SEAN

He sits there quietly, keeping his thoughts, information, ideas, and questions to himself. No hand-waver he! The teacher is nervous. Why doesn't he *participate?* She tells Mom and Dad that Sean is a nonjoiner, not interested, withdrawn.

Is he learning? they ask. Well, it's hard to say, she answers.

Does he do his workbook right? they ask. Does he do his work on the board right? Does he pass his tests?

Oh yes, she confesses, to all those queries.

So, he is doing all right. Let him do it his way. Don't make him self-conscious about his reserve or shyness. Eventually he'll learn to be as outgoing as he needs to be—but not if he's badgered.

This is close to my heart. I remember when I was in fifth grade going from New York to Massachusetts for the first time on the train. My parents had bought a farm. It was an exciting prospect for a city child. I took my geography book with me, and riding up along the Connecticut River I looked for towns and changing contours of land, and when we got there I knew exactly where I was on the map.

Next week my teacher complained to my mother that I didn't seem interested in learning. My mother couldn't believe her. She told her about my trip with the geography book to illustrate my enthusiasm. It didn't really convince that teacher. She couldn't bear my nonparticipation. I was too quiet for her.

It is not American to be retiring. However, there are retiring kids and they do all right in the long run, as I have. Your retiring kid will, too, if you don't worry about him. He'll grow up to be as aggressive as he needs to be if he isn't made self-conscious about his manner. Perhaps he won't get all A's. Some teachers automatically lower kids' marks if they don't speak up, raise their hands to volunteer, participate in discussions, etc. But is it *really* important for children to get A's in grade school? The important question to ask is, "Is he learning? Is he interested?" If he is, stop thinking about what's wrong with him and show approval. The surer he gets to be, the sooner he'll muster the courage to participate when it is important.

THE DORMOUSE

I remember a child whom the teacher always called the dormouse. Sometimes she seemed to be asleep.

Sometimes she was looking out the window. Sometimes she actually would wander over to the window to look out. But, whenever the teacher called on her, she answered promptly and well. It was maddening to the teacher. Like the dormouse in *Alice in Wonderland,* she was there and she wasn't. Lots goes on in the mind and imagination of the dormouse. Unless she or he is really out of it—not learning, not taking in what is going on, not responsive when called on—let him be.

Teachers have all kinds of rationalizations for labeling the different children abnormal, and ordering them altered, fixed, remodeled, corrected, treated, what have you.

They are likely to say, "If everyone in the class did what he is doing, how could I possibly teach?"

What they don't stop to think is that EVERYONE doesn't, wouldn't, and won't. *Everyone is different!* Everyone is not the same. Everyone—in spite of our fantasies—is not all-American, nor fast, slow, noisy, unquenchable, restless, retiring, brilliant, athletic, and so on. If teachers spent less time worrying about getting every child to act like every other child and all of them to make things easiest for her, then slow, quiet, restless, shy, bold, outspoken, would all come right along. No worry anywhere!

As common as the fallacy of the NORMAL CHILD is the fallacy of

2. THE PERFECT PARENT

One reason parents fall into the NORMAL CHILD trap is that they have been brainwashed into believing that parents should be perfect. How can you tell when you are? Easy, you have a perfect child. So, if a teacher says, "Your Jennifer seems a bit slow," or "Can we do something about teaching Frank to calm down?" or "Pammy to wake up?" or "Sue to get over her shyness?" or "Sarah to follow instructions?" parents instantly get on the defensive.

"So, my child is not normal, all-American. What have I done wrong?"

Instead of listening carefully to whatever criticism or comment a teacher makes; or even thinking about whether it is accurate and valid, let alone important, they begin to worry, and wonder, "What have I done now?"

No matter who says parents should be perfect they can't be. You, too, are only human. Even if you were godlike, all-powerful, and could act and react perfectly every waking and sleeping moment of your child's life, you would absolutely be unable to change him into the mythical American construct—the NORMAL CHILD. But, by constantly trying and failing, you change him into a nervous, self-conscious, insecure little wretch.

The PERFECT PARENT trap follows logically from the

3. PERFECTIBILITY FALLACY

Both follow from the torrent of advice to parents that has flowed with the force and reliability of Old Faithful for two generations or more. Distilled from the experts' observations, random samples, memories of their own childhoods plus the recollections revealed on their couches by free-associating patients, and random samples, it is dispensed as the WORD on what children feel from birth to the age of consent; and how to turn it all positive.

Child development experts are not alone responsible for the doctrine of perfectibility—let's be fair. We have simply extended it from the world of American mechanical-technical genius. But, thinking up an assembly line to produce canned tomatoes is one thing. Using the same techniques for improving babies is another.

The variables are simply too numerous. In fact, it might be just as disastrous to try to perfect all children into all-American as it would be to make them all five-foot-two at ten—then using surgical correction to bring the deviants into line.

It is one thing to use your dominant position as a parent to bring up children to get along in the world—i.e. to be generally social-minded, and capable of independence and responsibility for others, within the framework of their individual capacities and interests. It is quite another to expect or even want them to be like everyone else—otherwise known as all-American, normal, the PERFECT CHILD.

The PERFECTIBILITY FALLACY, if you get caught in it, makes children unhappy with themselves, unhappy with you, and, in extreme cases, unable to function at all. Work with what you have. The better you learn to love him or her as is, the more likely he or she will be to have a good life. Isn't that what parents—nice parents, anyway—really want?

Another awful consequence of the PERFECT PARENT-PERFECT CHILD trap is that teachers fall into it along with parents—or even all by themselves. They, too, feel that they will get bad marks unless all their students are perfect. When they aren't, teacher gets caught in all sorts of other traps.

PASSING THE BUCK

If something goes wrong and a child does not fit the all-American formula, teacher blames the parents. It's more comfortable than acknowledging something wrong with her teaching. Parents, for their part (not wanting to be responsible, either), throw the blame right back to teachers.

This is the buck-passing trap. The way out is for parent and teacher to look each other straight in the eye and start analyzing the situation. Find out whether the child has a problem, or, indeed, whether the problem is simply that parents and teacher are busy blaming each other for something that doesn't even exist. You may discover that the child, in fact, is doing very well for him, even though he is not the all-around top-flight model everyone prefers. But you may discover that a real problem does exist. In that case you don't want to keep passing the buck back and forth. You want to dig in and see if you can resolve it before it mushrooms.

NO SEE 'EM

Another way to avoid the awful burden of responsibility for not being the perfect parent or teacher is to fall into the NO SEE 'EM trap. Teachers and parents both are very susceptible.

"My child is not learning to read," a parent will complain.

"He'll read when he's ready. Don't be so anxious!

He'll sense it. Then he'll get fearful and develop a real problem," teacher says.

Or, "My child doesn't seem to have any friends."

"Really?" the teacher says. "I think everyone respects Sam. I can't see what you mean."

"I mean no one ever asks him to play at their house and he doesn't seem to have any friends to ask here."

"Oh, I don't think so. The children are all very friendly."

The implication, spoken or not, is that the teacher thinks the mother is imagining things. It's no help.

"Joanne is beginning to stutter," another mother reports. "She keeps asking for reassurance whenever she does anything. Do you think there is any strain in school that may be making her anxious?"

The teacher says, "She seems perfectly happy. I don't hear her stutter." Another brush-off.

Parents can play the same game. We are all afraid of problems, especially when we don't know what causes them or how to erase them. The pressure to make perfect children creates false problems, and demands that we solve them. Denial appears at first the best way to handle them. The trouble is, however, that once in a while a problem is real. It doesn't go away by being ignored.

Parents of one of the little boys who is in our study have been playing blind to a true social problem ever since he started school. The teacher pointed it out. We noticed he was excessively shy when we saw him, and heard that he tended to tattle to teacher when he got into fights with other children in his nursery school group. The teacher had discussed it with the mother. She said she thought that, together, they could find ways to build up Stefan's ego so he could stand on his own and get along with his classmates. Mother didn't agree. She preferred to play blind.

"Stefan is all right. It's just that the other children are bullies. They pick on him."

The same thing happened in first grade, and Stefan's mother played blind again. Now Stefan is in third grade —the perfect victim. The other children tease him, hide his things, make fun of the way he does everything, from reading to playing catch.

When we talk to teachers about him, they always say the same thing. "We can't get Stefan's mother to see what's happening. She always blames the other kids, so there is nothing we can do to help Stefan change his ways."

Stefan's mother is so defensive about a possible flaw in her son that she can't see the teachers' efforts as anything but critical. She can't accept help because she can't acknowledge needing it. She can't face a child with a problem, so she pretends it is not there and it grows and grows.

Lee, a little girl whom I have followed from infancy, has a learning problem. She's been developing it right from the beginning of school. She does not do her work. She is lazy, impatient, distractible, and finds it hard to keep her mind on one task for very long at a time. We knew all that when she was a few months old. At that time one of our staff who made a home visit reported that Lee was unusually sensitive to noise and motion for her age and that her eyes darted from one direction to the other constantly, even when the observer tried to hold her attention with the flashlight or a rattle. These observations suggested that Lee might become a distractible child. We didn't expect anything serious or even out of the ordinary. The problem is becoming serious simply because her parents refuse to face it. They play blind and turn down every teacher's plea for help. When Lee was in grade one they told her teacher that open classroom teaching wasn't giving her enough discipline. In grade two they said her problem in learning developed because the child next to her talked all the time. They couldn't explain why *that* child was learning anyway. In grade three they blamed Lee's failure on a punitive teacher. Next year it will be something else.

Parents and teachers get caught in traps when they make unreasonable demands on themselves and their children. You can make it much easier for yourselves and your child if you stop trying to make him something he isn't, to fit that all-American stereotype of what's normal.

THE OVERUNDERSTOOD CHILD

Some parents use the push, pull, knead, mold approach. Others believe in the *laissez-faire* method. They realize that raising a perfect child is serious business. Therefore they bone up. They read enough psychiatric literature to know that adult problems have their roots in childhood unhappiness.

Childhood unhappiness, they figure, comes from stifling the good, true, and beautiful innate bent of the child, warping its natural tendency to grow and flourish. They act as if one tear made a trauma and go about child rearing in a pussyfooting manner. They react with fear and trembling to every whimper of the newborn. By the time the child is walking and talking they are phobic about frustrating him.

Anticipating, preventing, and relieving frustration become the focus of parent-child relations.

This is bad enough in the preschool years. In extreme cases, parents become vassals to an infant king, who regulates their eating, sleeping, and leisure patterns, household decoration (accident-proof and indestructible), as well as his own life, with the quiver of a chin. It is only when the child ventures forth into the real world and parents have to speculate in absentia on the cruelties that might be inflicted, that overunderstanding really sets in.

Psychoanalysis is superficial compared with the depth probing that goes on in the overunderstanding home. Working on the assumption that happiness is perfection, a child's simple nonsmile or silence can be grounds for alarm and cause for action.

Some random examples:

Johnny looks solemn at breakfast on the morning of his first day in kindergarten. Parents exchange anxious looks. Mother begins presenting a beefed-up version of what lies ahead that makes kindergarten sound like a circus. When Johnny gets there, he takes one look, bellows, "Where are the animals?" And discovering there are none, sobs, hits his mother, and says, "You said there were animals." It takes four weeks to get him to go to plain ordinary kindergarten in the plain ordinary way.

A year passes. Johnny's mother has her first conference with his first grade teacher. The teacher says Johnny draws pictures in his workbook and doesn't follow the instructions. Would Mother please try to help him learn to do the work that is expected at home? Mother tries. Johnny cries. Mother decides a. the work is too hard b. Johnny is too creative c. Johnny will learn when he is mature enough d. the work is too easy and Johnny is bored e. the teacher is impossible.

Meanwhile Johnny does as he pleases.

Four years later Johnny is the class clown, trouble-maker, or sad sack, depending on what kind of personality he had to begin with. He has a repertory of excuses for every criticism leveled at him: "Joe did it." "You didn't explain it right." "I don't feel good."

He has no friends. He is not learning very well.

His parents remain hoveringly attentive. They are sure that another school would fix everything—an understanding, child-centered school. However, the understanding, child-centered school says Johnny is too immature for their groups. Johnny's parents go into analysis to find out what they have done to frustrate the natural florescence of the perfect child. The only trouble is that Johnny may be beyond redemption by the time they get the answer.

I remember a scene from my own childhood. I was quietly crying in a corner behind the kitchen door. Interestingly enough, I can't remember what I was crying about. I do remember that I was getting tired of it all, was about to stop, and already had my mind on joining my sister who was catching fireflies outside in the late August dusk.

Just then, my aunt walked in and asked me what was the matter. I didn't answer. She asked my mother who said, "Let her alone. She's all right."

Instead, my understanding aunt started to comfort and question. I obligingly started to sob all over again. Even as I did, I remember wishing she'd let me alone so I could get out to play.

To me this illustrates how seriously most children take the normal frustrations of life. If they could not absorb frustration and learn from it, they could never survive. Frustration teaches them—before they can understand why—to avoid physical danger. Fire, traffic, angry dogs and cats are obvious examples. And frustration teaches them the rudiments of getting along in life at a very tender age, before they know why: to go to bed when it is time; keep hands off the breakables; take care of books; not to kick or bite or scream to get what you want.

Does enforcing such demands traumatize children? On the contrary, it teaches them that parents can control —for them—the feelings they already know are unacceptable. Parental control is the first step toward self-control. It makes it possible for them to get along in a group so they won't be really traumatized later on by social ostracism, when their classmates avoid them. It teaches them to learn by following instructions so they will be ready to learn from their teachers when they start school.

Equally important, it enables parents to maintain fairly equable relations with each other and the child, and still survive. Overunderstanding makes child rearing so exhausting that getting through the day's work, while allowing the child to act at will, often ends in tears, howls, and total rejection of one's offspring.

Frustration is far less traumatic. Reasonable restrictions and demands may be temporarily frustrating for children but they have positive value. They teach children to cope with the world and their own feelings and give them the security of knowing that their parents have the strength and assurance to protect them in a world they know they cannot manage themselves.

The real frustration and trauma, in fact, come from making demands on children which they cannot meet. Asking a child to decide what is best for him at an early age must be at the top of the list of impossible parental expectations.

Children have a right to learn about reality from their parents. If you protect them from everything negative, you give them a false picture of the world. If, for example, you reject a child's problem in school by blaming it on the teacher, you keep him from discovering that he can overcome difficulties.

If you insist on complimenting him indiscriminately for every paper, artwork, athletic performance, he will get a phony idea of his abilities, and no experience in judging his work or himself. Worse, if he's perceptive, he'll recognize your comments are valueless and decide that 1. you don't take him seriously enough to pay attention to what he is doing, or 2. you think so little of his effort that you are afraid to tell him the truth.

If you shield him from possible unpleasant experiences—tests, trips with other children, exposure to competition, you make him just as fearful as if you pushed him into things and demanded that he come out first. If you make a production of every scratch, imagined scratch, serious injury, physical or emotional, he never learns to discriminate between big and minor, and deal with his feelings accordingly. He may become obsessively preoccupied with avoiding pain or oblivious of feeling.

If you anticipate his responses; analyze his expressions, actions, and reactions; probe his motives constantly for clues to negative thoughts, unconscious fears, or incipient problems, you rob him of privacy.

You don't give him a chance to look at himself, approvingly or critically; make his own judgments and corrections; set his own goals for self-improvement, and finally become his own man or woman. You fiddle with him until he feels he is not himself at all. The result can be rebellion or alienation.

Fortunately most children recover from their over-understanding parents. When they go out into the real world, a sixth sense tells them it's wiser to play the game of the world than their parents' game and they find out how to get along on their own.

The child who suffers is the one who is temperamentally least adaptable to start with. Overprotective parents never give him the practice he must have to develop minimal facility at getting along in the ever-changing reality of everyday life.

Don't be afraid to be parents. Children need to know that adults are in charge.

THE DATEBOOK CHILD

Parents who feel obligated to produce perfect children spare them no experience that might be enriching. The perfect child is the all-around child. Therefore enrichment comes from all directions. This leads to a very full calendar. Monday it is music. Tuesday is dancing. Wednesday is horses. Thursday, arts and crafts. Friday is judo or religion, or typing, sewing, cooking, carpentry. You name it. DATEBOOK has it somewhere in his program of physical fitness, cultural advancement, social and moral uplift.

To squeeze it all in, he may have to skip friends, play, homework, daydreaming, or a do-nothing minute or two— Whoever heard of that! Certainly not the DATEBOOK child. He is so busy scurrying from one activity to the next he can hardly tell a potter's wheel from a riding ring.

What's wrong with it? Nothing at all, if it suits the child and he enjoys it.

Lots if 1. his frenzied round of activity overtires him, keeps him from enjoying the main business of childhood —learning to learn, learning to get along with people and develop interests, hobbies, and friends of his own.

Or 2. if strings are attached. For example, Mother says, "I gave you those boxing lessons and you aren't getting anywhere." Or Daddy says, "You asked for drums and you never practice." "You wanted to play tennis. Now you'll finish the course I've paid for." "You've been going to dancing school for five years and no one ever asks you to dance. It's a waste of money."

Or 3. if children are so showered with opportunities, advantages, and experiences that they literally don't know where to turn.

Empty moments—in fact empty hours—give them the chance to fantasize, consider, reconsider what they want to experiment with. Overstuffing with opportunities—generated largely by parents—is like overstuffing them with food. It takes away the appetite. It turns children off everything. It mechanizes them the way overunderstanding does. It robs them of the chance to make up their own minds about what they'd like to try, and dibble and dabble their way to mature taste, judgment, and interests.

Dilettantism is appropriate for children. It is different from the apathetic picking up and dropping of interests that comes from being overwhelmed with opportunities.

Children, of course, need opportunities to try sports, creative work, and social activities. But a little goes a long way—particularly in the preadolescent years. Be sparing is my advice. And don't expect much. Children are in no better position to know whether they'll like piano, for example, before they've tried it, than they can judge an attractive-looking olive before they taste it. Nine times out of ten the piano will be discarded just as the olive will be—unfinished. Don't pressure, too much. Be prepared. Borrow or rent an instrument if you have none. Don't sign up for a year of lessons in advance. Try a trial month or so before deciding, and discuss it first before you sign up for additional lessons.

Insisting that a bored, untalented piano student finish a year of daily practice sessions and weekly lessons will gain neither of you anything. The memory of discomfort, in fact, might keep a child from ever risking another activity that might really interest him.

I have seen children who are afraid to express interest in anything for fear they'll be committed to a lifetime course of study. Enrichment, yes! Forced feeding or overstuffing, no!

This may be a bit off the subject, but pertinent. Don't be too fulsome in your praise of what turns out. It's as terrifying to a child as being tied to activities he's merely expressed a passing interest in. Children who paint a pretty picture once and get showered with compliments may find the pressure to keep up the standard of achievement they think their parents expect so heavy that art becomes more work than fun. Play it cool.

Social activity may be handled in the same way as cultural enrichment. Some parents are after friends and social success as one more form of enrichment. My advice is the same. Don't push your child to be busy, busy. Let him decide—even at the nursery school age—whom he wants to play with and when; and whose houses he wants to visit. Use your common sense about tailoring this general advice to the particular child.

A shy, cautious child who thinks twice before trying

a new kind of candy, even, is going to be very hesitant about visiting other children, or playing in a group where there are any strange faces. You would want to see that he gets fairly regular exposure to new people and new places—even if you have to go with him for support at first—so that he will gradually learn to get along more easily and comfortably in life.

On the other hand you would probably want to enforce some empty time for a child who is constantly looking for someone to play with and always restlessly looking for something else to do. With your help he can learn to play quietly by himself; learn to be more reflective and selective about people and activities, and gradually become more self-sufficient.

COMPETITION

Competition is a little like motherhood. You just don't go around finding fault with it.

Maybe the very fact that we have accepted it for so long has closed our eyes to some of its drawbacks. At any rate I have some questions.

The other night a Latin professor I was talking to said he thought the "whole trouble" with this generation of young people stems from the fact that they didn't have to compete when they were children.

"They were allowed to learn as they please," he said. "And now that they have to compete in society they're afraid. That's why they drop out."

I don't agree. In fact, I think too much competition, too soon, rather than too little, too late, is what makes people unable to compete for the credentials and opportunities they need to get on with the work they really want to do in adult life.

Many so-called dropouts are not necessarily afraid to compete, but uninterested in the prize the professor considers valuable—"Making it" in the conventional sense. They say they don't like what success has done to their competitive parents and they don't want that kind of living for themselves. The kind of individuality some of the younger generation possess may make them better able to compete when they want to than many of their more conventional peers.

Emphasizing competition—showing serious concern about how well children behave, perform, rank in comparison with their classmates, friends, brothers and sisters—can, in my opinion, be very destructive.

Little children are tough characters—much tougher than parents in recent decades have been led to believe, but they are not invulnerable. Their newness and helplessness make them unsure and dependent. In the first years when they are just finding out what they are here for and how to get along, grown-ups' reactions tell them how they are doing. If their parents and teachers guide, encourage, and support their efforts to learn, develop skills and strength, according to their particular abilities, their innate push for growth and the pleasure and comfort they get from pleasing the grown-ups they love and depend on keep them moving forward.

Gradually, as they develop mastery and learn to assume some responsibility for themselves, the confidence that came initially from their parents' support and approval becomes *self*-confidence. With it, they gradually gain a sense of who they are. When they know who they are and what they want and have confidence that they are capable human beings, then they will have the will and courage to compete when they need to, to achieve what is important to them in life.

However, when the approval and encouragement they need is conditional upon their doing better than their friends and classmates or brothers and sisters—regardless of whether they are able to do better or not—they worry. "Can I, can't I? Will I, won't I?"

And, instead of going about the daily work that is play, and play that is work of early childhood, comfortably, they get edgy, unsure, and anxious. They are distracted from learning and developing easily and smoothly, and learn to concentrate instead on the irrelevant business of doing what will win adults' approval.

Different children are affected to a greater or lesser degree, of course, depending on temperament and abilities. But competitive upbringing almost never helps any child.

Next time you find yourself asking your fourth-grader about his marks, or sports, or friends, stop and think about this. Does your question about where he stands in the class, what he did in the game, or how he's getting along in the popularity contest make him happy? Does he answer eagerly? Does your concern make him interested in studying more carefully? Does it make him care about *what* he is learning? Does it encourage him to explore and develop real interests that may lead to future study? Does concentrating on performance make him more confident in himself? Or does your concern make him worry about his abilities not only to perform but to have your approval and love?

Do you remember what it was like to have to worry about whether you were doing well enough to earn your parents' or teacher's approval? Can you remember what it felt like when you failed to measure up in their eyes, against brothers or sisters, classmates or friends?

I don't have to remember. I see and hear what it is like every day, watching and listening to the children I take care of in the pediatric clinic at Bellevue, and in my private practice.

Here are a few examples that are fresh in my mind.

1. Six-year-old Sally is reading a book to herself. Her little sister Sue is playing with cars on the floor. Their mother calls from upstairs and asks Sally to turn off the hose. Before Sally stops reading and puts down the book Sue has run and done the job. Grandmother smiles sweetly at Sue. "Sally," she says to her older granddaughter, "Sue is just a baby and she can do things better than you can. What's the matter with you?"

Sally doesn't say anything. Her grandmother rattles on, cooing over Sue. Sally quietly slips out of hearing.

2. Jonathan, aged twelve, is in the rush-rush math class. His teacher wanted him there. He comes home each day with furrowed brow, complaining to his mother that he can't keep up. He says they are going so fast that he doesn't really understand the work. He is a good student. He loved arithmetic. Now he hates it. He is beginning to lose interest in school altogether. The teacher says he seems tired and asks if he is getting enough sleep. His mother explains the problem and asks to have him moved to a less advanced math group. The teacher insists he is quite able to do the work. She suggests that his mother is overprotective. Jonathan worries out the year.

3. David is a very enthusiastic, bouncy little boy. The teacher in first grade "science" is telling about frogs. She goes on and on, reading from a natural history encyclopedia. He is resting his head on his arms on the desk, daydreaming. Suddenly he sits up and waves his hand. The teacher ignores him. Finally he interrupts her. "My father showed me the whole thing in my grandma's

pond," he says. "It's got lots and lots of real eggs and little, little tadpoles, right now."

The teacher looks very cross. "David, you are not listening. Now you won't be able to do your work and you will have a very poor report. We are talking about frogs. We are not talking about your grandmother's pond. Now what do frogs do when it is cold?"

Before David has a chance to tell her, because he *does* know, she goes on. "You don't know because you were not listening. Carol, I'm sure you can tell me."

The light goes out of David's eyes. He puts his head back down on his arms and begins to suck his thumb.

4. Joe switches schools in second grade. The new school is very much stricter than the old one about reading. He is way behind. Everyone reads the same book. The teacher goes around the class, having each child read one sentence at a time out loud in order. Joe has never read in public. He can't follow. When it is his turn he has to have help finding the place. He fumbles and falters. The teacher is patient. But the other children's hands wave all around him. They begin to shout the words before he can read them. He gets red. He tries not to cry. He complains every morning that his stomach hurts.

5. At the beginning of the year Betty's nursery teacher finds that she can't understand what the child is saying. She thinks Betty will have trouble getting along in the group. Betty and her mother came to see me. Betty did have a very slight language problem. I gave her mother a few simple suggestions for helping her at home and recommended some sessions with a speech therapist. I emphasized that the problem could be easily corrected if it were attended to before Betty started school.

The mother seemed to want more assurance that

Betty's speech would be normal. Before she left I went over the instructions, including the recommendation that she get speech therapy for a few months. Then, once more I said I was sure the problem would go away if she took care of it right away.

Three years later mother and child were back. Betty's first grade teacher had reported that Betty's problem was preventing her from learning to read.

I asked whether Betty had had speech therapy and the mother looked at me in astonishment. "Why should she have speech therapy, when you said it would go away?" she asked.

She apparently had no recollection of my instructions. I outlined a new, more stringent corrective program. The mother seemed to listen and even took notes, but I suspect she will again do nothing. Before she left she said, "Betty is as smart as any of them. She can learn if she wants to."

Betty hung her head.

6. Tim is eight. He didn't make the Little League team. His father is very upset. Every night he has Tim practice with him as soon as he gets home. He has to coax, almost command, before Tim reluctantly goes for the gloves and ball. His father comments on every catch and every throw. Every time Timmy misses a ball his father sounds more impatient. Timmy begins to throw wilder and wilder. "You're not even trying," his father says. "You're never going to get on *any* team. What are you, an idiot?"

Timmy runs off in tears. "I won't try out even if you make me. I hate baseball."

7. Joanne is an average (in marks) third grade student. Her teacher, though, finds her a great addition to the class. She is very curious. Her questions and obser-

vations about prehistoric times, which they are studying, stimulate the other children's interest and participation. She is a catalyst.

Her parents expect her to get A in everything just like her older brother. She gets 70's and 60's in spelling. The teacher is not concerned. She is confident that Joanne will learn to spell better as she begins to write more. With her enthusiasm and interest she will certainly do that in a year or two.

The parents have a daily ritual. Both children present their papers for inspection every evening and the parents deliver little lectures on what they find. Brother gets the praise. Sister gets the blame.

One day Joanne's spelling mark has been changed from 60 to 80 and two of her four misspelled words have been corrected—not very skillfully. When her father sees her paper he slaps her and sends her to her room.

A few days later the teacher sees her looking at her neighbor's paper. She spells all her words correctly and gets 100.

What are these competitive parents doing to their children?

Sally's grandmother might have praised her for being so interested and advanced in reading at such an early age. She could have simply reminded her to pay more attention when her mother asks her to do something. Instead she made fun of her for not being as eager and quick as her baby sister at performing an unimportant chore.

Jonathan, an enthusiastic math student, becomes an anxious one. Instead of learning happily at his own sure pace, he begins to lose confidence in himself and his ability. If his mother had backed up the pushy teacher, the pressure to learn more, faster might have seriously interfered with his interest in learning at all.

David who has learned all about frogs, firsthand, is getting an early warning signal that memorizing a teacher's words is more important than learning for yourself and understanding what you have seen and heard.

Joe finds it so painful *not* knowing as much as his classmates that he hasn't got the persistence and stamina to hang in and learn how to read.

Betty has been actually prevented from learning. Her mother finds it easier to blame her child for not trying than to face the fact that she has a problem and correct it so Betty can learn. Betty's mother has to compete, through Betty, in the perfect child sweepstakes. Perfect children don't have problems.

Tim is learning to hate baseball. Much worse, he is learning to hate himself and see himself as a failure.

Joanne is learning that her inquisitive, creative mind and enthusiasm about everything around her are far less important than getting a perfect report card. She is finding out how to cheat and pretend instead of developing through her innate strengths.

Not every child is affected this deeply, of course. Some are less sensitive by nature. Criticism and disapproval don't bother them so much. They can either ignore parents' and teachers' excessive demands, or brush off disapproval when they fail. In some cases the satisfaction they get from being successful in one area enables them to ignore disapproval for other failures. Many children are naturally so quick and able that they can please without trying.

The all-around, good student, good athlete, adaptable, able, attractive child, known as a "good kid," seems to be immune to the ill effects of the competitive way.

But I am not sure he escapes altogether, either. All too often, I feel a child of this nature with his incredible human potential gets squeezed into a very tight mold when he has to win-win-win! Before he is in his teens, he makes praise, marks, medals, and records the object of life. In his determination to be best and gain the official stamp of approval at home and school he may never have the freedom, or playtime, or idle time to develop the academic, creative, and intellectual interests which, in the long run, might bring him greater fulfillment and accomplishment than all-around success.

More remarkable, however, than the fact that some well-endowed youngsters can escape the immediate ill effects of a competitive environment, is the number of perfectly normal children who are vulnerable.

I have a vivid memory of Allan. His parents asked me to help when he suddenly refused to go to school shortly after the start of fourth grade. He was bright, attractive, and humorous. His parents seemed affectionate and understanding, and, of course, they were terribly concerned about the full-blown school phobia that had developed in their apparently happy son overnight.

It was some time before I found the explanation. They were clearly not responsible. They turned out to be just what they appeared to be on our first meeting. They had two sons. They were quite clear and correct about what those boys were like in temperament and ability. They weren't pushing to be better than each other or anyone else. They were satisfied with them just as they were.

I couldn't see how Allan's teacher could have brought on his trouble. She was pleasant and intelligent and made a point of suiting her demands—which were not rigid—to each of her student's abilities. She was almost as upset at what had happened as Allan's parents.

It was nine-year-old Allan who finally unlocked the secret. In spite of being a popular boy he was a lousy athlete in a boy's school where team sports and athletic skill came first. He had made his peace with this situation because he was top student in his class. His obvious superiority as a scholar gave him enough clout to gain his classmates' respect and spare him the scorn usually reserved for nonathletes.

The week before his panic his teacher, hoping to shield her kids from anxiety, announced the annual achievement tests by saying they would tell her what ground the class needed to cover during the year. She made a point of repeating several times that the children's individual performance was not important.

Allan became convinced, then and there, that he was not going to come in first in those particular tests as he always had. He knew the teacher had said that the records were not important. That didn't matter. All records were important to Allan. He depended on being first in class to compensate for being a "dunce" in athletics. He became convinced that these particular tests would expose him. His classmates would discover that he was not REALLY number one in academic work. What he had feared from the day he started school would happen now. Instead of being one of the IN's making fun of the OUT's, which he had done with his classmates, he would be the OUT and the target of their teasing himself.

He could not face the prospect and he panicked.

Allan went back to school after a few weeks with a more reasonable attitude toward the importance of being top scholar, and a more sensible view of his own assets and liabilities. But he never did get over the memory of that panic. He had to make a conscious effort all through school to keep from running away from the fear of not coming in first every time he was faced with a new group of his peers. Years later, when he was a freshman in college, he told me that he survived the first weeks only by reminding himself of what we had worked out together when he was nine. "Remember, in a month you'll find yourself completely at home. You are not going to be best. You don't have to be. Be yourself. You'll make friends and in a month you'll feel completely at home."

Fortunately Allan's parents were quite satisfied with him and his progress toward growing up. Without them I don't believe he could have learned to cope with the fear of failure he developed in that competitive school.

I may be laboring the dangers of forcing children to compete for approval and respect during their early years. We are living in a competitive society. We have to get used to competing in order to get almost anywhere we might want to go. However, I don't feel that explains or justifies the widespread pressure on children to put winning first at the earliest possible moment.

Studies by child development experts and educators tell us that supportive, interested parents are a most powerful stimulus for learning. But we act as if we believed little children would just sit there and remain helpless, if we didn't make it clear that we like them better for doing better than the next guy, and less when they come out behind.

Like the professor of classics I mentioned in the beginning, we sometimes seem terribly worried that unless kids learn to huff and puff early, they may never huff and puff at all. This may reflect on our own childhood conditioning for competition.

When children learn that parental approval and affection depend on how they do at an age when they are still so young that they are not sure of what they *can* do, they react with some degree of anxiety. This can develop into an underlying, persistent fear that they might some day be unable to act at all; even a half fear, half wish that they might somehow escape the constant need to win in order to get the support and approval of parents, by some act of fate—accident or illness.

By the time they are grown up this becomes a nagging worry about making it in the world, which they extend to their children. They fear that the children will not make it, either, unless they push. So, the cycle repeats itself. Parents use the very tactics that have made them anxious, in order to activate their children. And, because the pattern is so ingrained, they sometimes do not even know what they are doing.

I was talking to a guidance teacher recently about a child whom we agreed was failing because of plain, simple fear of trying. At the end of our discussion she said, "If only parents would let their children choose what they want to try next."

I knew just what she meant before she went on. "This child's mother loads her with books she can't read, puzzles and games that are much too advanced for her. The child has been straining and failing all her short life to do things her parents require in order to satisfy themselves that she is 'gifted.'"

Perhaps indirect competitive ploys are more common than the old-fashioned Kennedy-style tactics of raising children to be best at whatever they try. I know one mother who wouldn't think of saying anything but a neutral, "That's fine," whenever she sees her daughter's report card, whatever the report card shows. However, she reviews the child's homework every night and makes her stay up, no matter what, until each assignment is letter perfect.

I have seen parents whose self-image is dependent on how they rank in every department of life, from dress to weight to income. The kids are studiously told to study for learning's sake—not for marks. But, their mother checks with their friends to see how their marks compare. The children are just another of the performances by which the parents rate themselves. The parents of Betty, described earlier, are an example. Betty's mother was so threatened by the possibility that her little girl would not do her credit in the successful child department that she could not even recognize Betty's minor language problem and correct it so the child could develop normally.

I must have seen literally hundreds of parents who wanted their children tested in order to establish that they were smart enough for some school or other that had turned them down on the grounds that the child would not be happy there—a euphemism that usually means the child is not strong enough intellectually, or temperamentally—in the school's opinion—to be successful there.

I try to persuade the parents that there is nothing to gain for the child by forcing him into an environment for which he is not suited. I suggest alternative schools and explain why the child will develop better in the long run with less pressure.

Many parents relax when they see that what they are doing is counterproductive for the child. But, often, having a child in the "best" school or camp is part of the parents' self-image, like owning a Cadillac. They have to have the best, and they blindly insist that the best is what they have. The child who does not meet the standards for the label obviously has a rough time.

Teachers are as susceptible as parents. They want to make good records and their students' performance is the best evidence of their ability. Like some parents, they may pay lip service to the principle of individual teaching for individual children. But, if they are anxious about their own status, they may concentrate on the kids who make the honor roll, get the science fair prizes, or make the Ivy League colleges.

What follows? The most promising students—usually the quickest, most articulate, most responsive—get the smiles, the coaching, and assistance. The quiet, careful, slower (not duller), get by-passed, hurried or impatiently dismissed when they try to participate or ask questions. The child who needs extra help to understand new material—unless he is durable and persistent—falls behind. The timid are hurt.

Then, when they don't make satisfactory progress, these students are explained away as unteachable, unmotivated, immature, brain damaged, or lacking in the family background for learning.

Nothing an individual parent can do is likely to have much influence on teachers like this. Because they make good records they are considered successful. Their principals support them. You can talk to them, urge more rational ways of motivating all the class to learn, try to explain your child's particular difficulty and ask for help. You may get a promise of co-operation, but, in practice, little will change. If you know your child is falling behind and you can't help him keep up, it is worth while trying to get him shifted to another teacher. But the only truly effective way to correct pushy schools is through a strong parent organization that can exert pressure on the administration to shift the educational emphasis from coaching prize winners to teaching all the children.

There is a great deal you can do at home, however, to minimize the effects on your children. You are the most influential adults they know. What you have made them feel is important; what you value them for is what they usually believe. No matter what age your child is now, stop for a minute and think what your day-in, day-out demands and expectations are teaching him about himself and about work.

Are you encouraging him to find out about what he likes, what he can do most easily, how to be patient and persistent about mastering suitable tasks that are hard at first? Do you enjoy his little successes? Are you usually casual about his failures? Does he seem to be developing increasing confidence in his abilities, and pleasure in learning—whether the lesson is eating with a spoon or Latin grammar? Is he beginning to have deep interests in work, hobbies, sports? Or is he easily discouraged by mistakes? Does he seem overconcerned when he can't do what his friends or siblings can? Does he lose interest when he is not first?

Listen to yourself. Do you ask questions that A. make your children feel you are interested in their lives? or ones that B. tell them you are worried about how well they are doing?

Here are some typical questions and comments to illustrate the difference:

A.	B.
I saw you playing catch with Roger yesterday. All your practice is really showing. You two are really good.	Hey, you haven't told me who got to be pitcher on the team. Did they drop you?

How do you like your new teacher, Sal? What is she like?	Does your new teacher like you?
I'm glad to see your science mark is going up, Peter. I know that if you would try to be more patient you would get interested, and I see you must be finding it easier. Am I right?	I don't like that C in science. You're a very bright boy, like your father. You should be getting A.
I was pleased to see your paper on the board at the meeting today. You must have done some reading to find out so much about the Brooklyn Bridge. Where did it all come from?	Why wasn't *your* paper on the board? I see Jim's was. He isn't any better than you are. I told you you should have done it over.
	Aren't you invited to Pat's party? I spoke to Helen today and she said Suzy was going.

American parents don't have to teach their children about competition. They absorb it with the air they breathe. By the time they are in high school they know that competition is the name of the game if they want any kind of sustained career.

Some people, like my classics professor, think that children will run away from competing unless they are inured to it from practicing it all their lives the way one practices typing—to master speed and skill. Quite the contrary. Some, of course, do compete effectively out of habit, and the ingrained need to win. But many successful young people compete well because winning is necessary to fulfillment of the plans they have laid for their lives.

They get their motivation from the support, encouragement, and guidance of parents and teachers and not from training in competition.

Children have a built-in urge to develop and master the skills their culture demands. Co-operative adults are all they need to keep them moving toward maturity. Parents provide the initial stimulus. Gradually, children make their parents' implicit and explicit demands their own, in a complex interactive process that goes on through the early years.

Parents naturally have to do more than exist. They should be models worth loving and—as children grow sophisticated enough to judge—worth following. They need to back up their demands with day-to-day training. Thus, a parent will encourage a lazy child to take more pride in his work. He may instruct, command, correct, drill, discipline. He will reinforce his lessons with rewards—from simple approval to special surprises. He tries to encourage success without dwelling on failure. He respects effort, even when results are not exciting. Generally, he conveys the impression that the child has a viable future no matter how dim present prospects seem.

You may see this as encouraging children to compete with themselves. So be it. There is a very clear distinction in my mind between teaching a child to develop his best abilities as well as he can and encouraging him to try to beat the next guy. Competition encourages children to ignore themselves, and work indiscriminately for winning. Coincidentally, it teaches them that what does not win is no good. Teaching children to make the most of themselves; encouraging them to know their strengths, recognize their weaknesses, and explore and develop their own interests provides the foundation, I feel, for the confidence and judgment that will truly lead them to discover what they want in life and to be able to compete for it if necessary, when the time is right.

CHAPTER NINE

Q & A

Q. How can you keep kids from competing with each other? We have a daughter who has been struggling unsuccessfully since she was four to keep up with her older brother who has a natural talent for being "best" at everything. We think her hopeless struggle is beginning to interfere with development of her own individual strengths and interests. Every time she has something new to do she belittles herself before she even starts—"I'm no good at sports" or "I probably won't be able to."

A. Of course you don't want to deny or minimize your son's success. But you can try to help your daughter see that her brother is unusual—even among his classmates— so that she could hardly expect to keep up with him. Also try to help her see the importance and satisfaction she can get from learning at her own pace in her own style. Teachers sometimes compare younger children with brothers or sisters they have taught before. They may expect too much of her. If you explain the problem, perhaps they will be more careful to treat her as an individual with special qualities of her own.

I occasionally recommend sending siblings to different schools when the strain of keeping up with an older or younger child seems to be getting in the way of healthy growth.

More positively, think over the way you handle this daughter. You may find that you have put more emphasis on school performance than you realize. Pay more attention to your daughter's special abilities and she will pay less attention to her brother's.

Is she a hard, persistent, patient worker? Is she responsive and sensitive to you and her friends? Is she graceful, agile? Comment on her virtues when you can. If she has a particular interest in art, music, dance, tennis, or whatever, help her develop it, and let her know you value it.

Q. A nursery school teacher once told me that she would automatically avoid a school that insisted on admissions tests for three-year-olds. She thinks testing young children in a strange place with strange people is cruel and inhuman and could cause a test phobia later. She thinks observing a child in a play setting with other children is as revealing of development and personality as test results, and perhaps more useful. Do you agree?

A. Certainly it is totally unnecessary to test a normal three-year-old to find out how well he will fit into a nursery group. You can tell this very well, as you say, from observing him with his mother and at play with other children. However, testing need not be traumatic if the tester is skilled and sensitive. Three-year-olds usually enjoy tests, as a matter of fact. After all they are almost indistinguishable from the puzzles and toys and games with grown-ups that they have been exposed to since infancy.

Q. I don't see how you can expect children to be immune to the competitive atmosphere in most schools and camps. My ten-year-old son has been competitive from the day he first made friends and tried to beat his buddy to the top of the park jungle gym. He comes home every afternoon with stories about who was best at everything from social studies to ice cream consumption. He doesn't seem to care whether he's the winner, and he usually isn't, but he loves competing. He'll ask us to go over spelling words so he can get 100. He knows exactly what's wrong with his backhand, now that he's playing tennis, and makes us hit backhands to him as long as we can last. We try to cool it, but we can't. His brothers make fun of him for being an eager beaver but it doesn't have the slightest influence. We think he is doing more competing than learning.

A. I don't think you should take this too seriously. You have a very persistent, sociable kid who seems to like the sporting aspect of competition and is not the least threatened by how he stands. He is clearly enjoying the way he has chosen to go about work and play and is learning some good habits, such as diligence and patience, along the way. As he gets older he will undoubtedly become more deeply interested in some things than others and less concerned about being on the winning team every minute. Your guidance and encouragement of interests and aptitudes might help. Your questions about some of his competitive activity and its value might make him more discriminating. However, he may always be an individual who likes the contest more than the content of life. If so, he's lucky to be born into the right society for him.

Q. You seem to be against all competition for children. How do they learn to get along in the real world if they can't face competing with their peers in school?

A. I am against competition for young children. However, I do not mean to imply that I think they should be protected from the realities of life. It is one thing for a

child of eight, for example, to know how he stands, compared with his classmates, in reading, math, handwriting, spelling; to know that he is good-looking, slow at
running, good at climbing, a fair catcher—i.e. to have a
real picture of himself. It is another thing for him to be
afraid that unless he is best at reading, handwriting,
spelling, running, catching, looks, etc., his parents will
be disappointed, his classmates won't like him, and his
teacher will say he's not trying.

Competition in the latter instance discourages effort
and creates anxiety. It also sets children the impossible
goal of perfection instead of encouraging them to make
the most of what they are and who they are. Parents can
help children develop and improve their strengths and
overcome their weaknesses, at the same time enjoying
them as they are. This lays the foundation of confidence
and self-esteem that promotes maturity.

I would not worry too much about competition in
school under normal circumstances. Most children with
affectionate parents don't feel the need to compete twenty-
four hours a day just because they are in competitive
schools. Children can usually pick the area in which they
are interested in excelling and let the rest go by; or they
can ignore the whole competitive environment and dog-
gedly proceed at their own pace. I would encourage this.

Q. One of our children is almost paralyzed by tests.
She is a top student, yet she barely passes any test she
takes. We have always tried to make her realize that she
has nothing to fear. She knows, herself, that she is an
able student. What can she do?

A. Her test phobia may not have anything to do with
your demands and expectations. Many children have
stage fright before tests. They may lose their appetites,

get upset stomachs, diarrhea, or headaches. They study —even overstudy—until they are letter perfect on dates, facts, vocabulary, grammar, or whatever subject they are to be tested on. When they see the test they forget everything. When they finally get started and complete the test, they will go over it and decide all the answers are wrong, and change them—actually *making* them wrong.

I was test-shy myself, as a child. I had to get over it to become a doctor, and I learned a few tricks that helped. First: go over any test or exam quickly and pick the question that looks easiest to you. Start there. It works the way warming up does for an athlete. By the time you finish the easy question you are usually more relaxed and better able to face the rest of the test with your faculties under control. Second: when I had essay questions to answer I did not stumble over getting started. I began to write the first part of the subject that came to me. Then I went back to organize my material correctly.

These techniques helped me, but I was still in the bottom of my medical school class, in spite of better than average clinical skills and ability to express myself orally. At the end of my student days I resolved never to take another exam, no matter what gates it would open for me. I have stuck to it. I have never applied for a post that required a competitive examination.

I still get stage fright occasionally when I have to speak on a subject with which I am not completely familiar. I feel very comfortable talking on the work we have been doing for many years, and I never need more than a few topic words as an outline to make me feel secure. However, recently I had a recurrence of the old stage fright when I had to speak on some new research for the first time. The only way I could overcome it was to write down the whole talk, including the case histories, which I was afraid I would forget at the crucial moment.

If a child is so incapacitated by test phobia that he is in danger of being excluded from work he wants to do in life, I would recommend psychiatric treatment. The objective in such cases is to find out what is causing the paralyzing fear; then to explore the underlying reasons to help the child see his behavior in more realistic fashion.

Some children are temperamentally conditioned to be test-shy. The child who is naturally timid, shy, and eager to please is more fearful of exposing himself to the judgment of peers or adults than the happy extrovert. Many children, however, become excessively anxious because they have been conditioned—at home or at school—to put excessive importance on doing best at everything every minute.

As soon as a young person begins to recognize he is treating each test as if it were the one and only chance he has to prove himself, he begins to feel some relief. Simple coping methods like the ones I used as a student help build confidence, too.

Q. Don't you see any danger in overprotecting children from the realities of life? How can they find out what their strengths and weaknesses are if they don't compare their own performance with their schoolmates' and friends'?

A. They will do this, no matter what steps you take to minimize the importance of competition. Usually, they can handle that. It is only when you, as parents, measure their value by the way they compare with others, that they are distracted from learning and developing their capabilities. You encourage false values by judging them by the way they rank with their peers. It makes them try to beat their schoolmates, instead of learning and growing; try for tricky tactics and correct answers, rather than understanding and mastery.

Underplaying the value of competition does not shield children from its reality. You would be overprotecting them only if you *pretended* they were superior in a competitive situation when they were not; or deceived them into thinking they were more capable than they are; or intervened to get marks changed or prizes awarded, regardless of the merits. This kind of intervention would also convey the contradictory message that you were just as worried about results as their teachers and valued them chiefly by their marks.

10

THE UNDERACHIEVER

Parents can be proud of smart children. They can sympathize with ones who aren't first in the class. But the child who doesn't "live up to his potential" worries them, puzzles them and—yes—annoys a lot of fathers and mothers. Being an underachiever suggests not really *wanting* to do your best. This is a child, in parents' eyes, who could get good marks, could be successful. But, for some mysterious reason, he just doesn't seem to try.

In this society you're supposed to want to win. People who don't try to get ahead just don't make it. You don't laze into success. So it's not too surprising that parents get upset when a child is labeled an underachiever.

But, wait a minute! Don't panic if you find out from Johnny's teacher that he isn't doing as much as he's capable of. Underachievement means different things to different people. Find out what Johnny's teacher means. Then find out what measures she uses to decide that he is performing below capacity.

Underachievement is academic performance well below what a child's scores on standard intelligence tests would lead one to expect. It should not surprise a teacher if a child with average intelligence test scores does average or even below average classwork. But when one with high scores does barely passing or even failing work in all his subjects, he's definitely an underachiever.

There are many reasons for underachievement. Some are more serious than others. I don't take underachievement under certain circumstances as seriously as some parents and teachers do, but I think it is always well to find out what's behind it, without letting things drag too long. Sometimes there's nothing serious to worry about. But there are times when it is very important to start remedial action quickly. Under any circumstances underachievement is something to look into.

First, let's try to get some perspective. A child who *always* does his best whether he's smart, dull, quick, or slow is just as rare as the adult who "tries harder" every waking moment. We want to guard against expecting more in the way of application and effort from children than we would from ourselves.

One very bright little boy I knew got very tired of people saying after any test or paper: "Sammy, you could have done better. With your IQ you could have gotten 100." Or, "I expected an A+ from you on that paper."

He knew his IQ was 160, he'd heard it so often. One day when he was about nine he said to me, "I'm so sick of that number. Every time I don't get an A they bug me."

Sammy, like all of us, had different reasons at different times for not doing his best. He happened to be very busy—at that point—learning how to make friends who weren't awed by his intellect. And in my opinion, as long as he was busy learning and not bothering anyone else, he should have been let alone.

We can't expect uniform performance from children based on their IQ scores. Lots of different things determine how well a child does in school—among them taste, temperament, teacher-child relations, parent-child relations, intelligence, learning style, learning lags of various kinds, and personality problems.

I divide underachievers into the real and the pseudo-underachievers. Pseudo-underachievers are learning what they're supposed to be learning, all right. They're just not showing the superior performance, combined with effort, diligence, and total conscientiousness that parents and teachers want.

Some bright children turn off in second and third grade because they have learned the fundamentals so fast that they are careless about the drills and routine workbook exercises that take them over the same material again and again. They have no serious problem. The only danger is that if they go on too long with only half their attention and interest engaged, they may fall into lazy ways. Then, when they reach the point where education gets interesting to them they won't have the work habits and the mastery of fundamental skills that they need to cover material as fast as they want to.

I think good teachers and co-operative parents can keep bright kids from turning off in the early grades by seeing that they get enough stimulating and challenging experiences in school and at home to keep their interest in reading and thinking alive.

This is not as hard as it seems. Very, very few boys and girls get bored in the early grades because schoolwork and drills are too easy and too monotonous. Most little children enjoy drills, no matter how easy they are. They have an enormous appetite for success. They like the feeling that they are real experts at phonics and simple sums. As a matter of fact I think it's harder for children who don't learn easily to keep interested in school than it is for the ones who find school a breeze.

I don't recommend that teachers and parents make children who have learned the lesson go over and over the same ground just for the sake of discipline. But it isn't necessary to go to elaborate lengths to keep them on their toes every second. Usually they finish their work before the other children. It doesn't hurt them to sit and dream a little, or draw, or work on a special storybook of their own. For example, children like to cut out pictures from magazines, or draw their own, and then tell a story with them—printing captions under each picture (with teacher's help), then sewing the pages together to take home and read to parents and younger brothers and sisters. They like to read class library books in their extra time. It isn't necessary to push them to do more or harder problems, or encourage them to get ahead of the rest of the class.

I've noticed that ambitious parents are sometimes overeager about their children's scholastic progress. I've also noticed that the children, with uncanny sensitivity to their parents' hopes and fears, sense it. They get the feeling that a great deal is expected of them before they've even learned to read. It's frightening. It makes them feel that they have to perform, instead of just following their natural inclination to do their work at their own pace in their own way. They react just the way kids do when you interrupt some imaginative play they are deeply involved in. They get self-conscious, stop what they're doing, and wait for you to go away and let them alone.

Parents who think their children are whiz kids mistake this reaction for boredom. They think the kids are so smart that school is too easy for them, and they take immediate steps to beef up the work program at home and at school. The more steps they take the less interest the children show. Pretty soon, if parents talk about the children's superiority and boredom enough, the kids find they have a good excuse for not settling down to work. They do the bare minimum. They become underachievers because it is easier than living up to parents' great expectations. I think it's safe to say that children cope better with work that's too easy—especially in the first grades—than they do with parental pressure to be the smartest kid on the block.

Children who have intense, one-sided interests from a very early age are sometimes labeled underachievers—mistakenly, in my opinion. They are so involved in their own pursuits—whether bugs, sports, rocks, or music—that they tune out almost everything else most of the time.

One of our children used to bring home worried notes from his teachers saying that he didn't pay attention and wasn't doing what he should in class. We had confidence in his intellectual involvement because we saw him at work. He was a very private kind of child. He needed one friend, and that friend was a lot like him. While they were always together, they often played separately, pursuing their individual interests. Our son was busy every free minute, all year round, exploring the brooks and ponds and earth and vegetation around us and taking it all in.

When he wasn't exploring, he was thinking about what he had discovered. One night in the middle of dinner when he was about five, he said, "I know why fish swim so well. They practice a lot."

There wasn't any question in anyone's mind that he

could learn what his class was learning. He just happened to be more interested in learning something else. I'm not even sure—given his particular interests and ours —that he would not have learned the basic skills he needed for his later education through his own exploration and reading as well as he might have through the school curriculum. But that isn't always the case. Children who learn as they please, like the super-bright children who turn off through boredom, may get into bad work habits that interfere with later learning.

They may not become proficient in the skills they'll need. They may not learn to follow instructions, organize their work and their ideas so that they are ready for harder work when they get to it. They may not learn what they need to know about getting along and working with other people.

I don't think they should run that risk. It's as silly to let children ignore standards for performance in school as it is to let them ignore home standards, in the vague hope that eventually they'll do what everyone else does. The problem, however, is to find the balance between too much laissez-faire and too much pressure for conformity. I don't for a minute recommend trying to cast any child—and especially these strongly defined, intense characters—into a mold. In the first place I think it's a great loss to deprive society of the riches that come from individuality. Besides, it doesn't work with the children. Push these children with strong interests of their own too hard, and they tune out completely. Young people who have never developed any genuine commitments or goals have such serious trouble in life that it makes you appreciate involvement and commitment in the very young and try to cherish it.

How can you cope with children's indifference to the

normal school program? I start with the premise that best all-round performance is not a desirable goal to aim for with any child. It's more effective to pare your demands—asking only that children learn what is necessary for present and future welfare.

Children need to know what is taught in elementary school well enough so that they will have the skills to handle complex and challenging work when they come to it.

They should also learn to judge their assignments so that they know how to plan their work and get it done on time. Then, when they get to secondary school, where they are expected to work more independently, they'll have the knack.

They need to learn to behave so that they don't get in their own way, or interfere with their classmates' efforts to learn, or their teachers' efforts to teach.

They need support and encouragement for their own interests, and stimulation to broaden them.

It isn't as easy as it sounds to follow these principles. Parents constantly have to buck the prevailing social pressure to produce children who fit the conventional picture of success—bright, ambitious, well-rounded, socially attractive, popular.

To illustrate: A friend of mine has an obviously intelligent, lively son. He never did well in school. At least not well enough to meet her demands for achievement. She spent a great deal of time trying to push the child and cajole his teachers into getting better performance from him.

One year he had a teacher who simply would not accept the idea that more stringent measures should be taken to get Stevie to work. Exasperated, my friend finally said, "But, Mr. Jones, you know he doesn't do his best."

Mr. Jones looked her straight in the eye and said, "Do you? Does anyone? Maybe Steven isn't doing his best, but he's doing a great deal more than you can put on his report card and some day—if we don't beat his enthusiasm and curiosity out of him—he'll find an interest and dig in hard."

That's just what happened, too. Mr. Jones impressed my friend so deeply that she tried very hard to curb her demands for straight A performance from Steven. He began to work much harder and more intensely on what he liked, and squeaked by in the subjects he wasn't interested in.

By the time he was ten it was clear that he would spend his life doing something involving hand and eye —art, design, building, something like that. Periodically, his mother or father would nag him about Spanish vocabulary, or urge him to think about college, and there would be a period of high family tension with no visible results. He did go to college for one semester, but after the first two weeks he announced it was a waste of money and applied to art school on his own. He was accepted and has never been called an underachiever— even by his mother—since.

Steven's mother and father may not have handled him perfectly. But who does his best? They had the right idea and the right intentions. They were wise enough not to demand that he perform up to the level his IQ indicated was possible. They did require certain basic performance so that if he wanted to be an architect, for example, he could have fulfilled the requirements for admission to architecture school. But they didn't make learning such an excruciating and unpleasant experience that he balked at performance of any kind—tuning out even his innate interest in art and creation.

It's not easy to give parents specific advice about handling a child like Stevie, except to repeat those basic guidelines: Let him pursue his own interests as freely and intensely as he likes. Start from his interest to encourage wider study; and teach academic discipline. Set modest but firm standards for performance in school. Maybe equally important—enjoy and share his enthusiasms if you can.

True underachievers are held back by personality or learning problems. Shy children, for example, have trouble learning because they don't like to ask questions or recite. Restless, restive children fall behind sometimes because they don't stay put and concentrate long enough to understand new work when it is taught.

Two dismal practices of our school system are especially hard on shy children. We begin to test children's intelligence before they have had time to adjust to being away from home. Then we divide the sheep from the goats, with very questionable results. The "bright" ones get lots of praise and attention. The "dummies" are too often ignored or scorned.

The second bad practice stems from the first. Teachers often equate being bright with knowing the answer and acting eager. They are often impatient or indifferent with children who don't know the right answer, don't like to recite, or ask what they call "dumb" questions. How often have you heard a teacher say: "Now, class, let's tell Jim the *right* answer. Jimmy doesn't seem to have had time for his homework last night," or "Jimmy doesn't know how to listen, yet."

This approach doesn't make children want to learn. It promotes ignorance. The shy, sensitive child is the most vulnerable. It doesn't matter whether he, or she, is smart, stupid, slow, fast. The mere possibility of making a mistake and being publicly or even privately rebuked, ridiculed, or corrected is so painful that it dominates his attention, blocking everything else out, and effectively preventing him from learning. It is literally impossible for some children to expose themselves to negative criticism or the possibility of failure.

This is just what happened to Barby. She did very well in first and second grades. In third grade her report cards changed. The teacher told her mother that Barby was not keeping up. She stuttered and stumbled when she was called on until "I have to ask someone else to help her answer," as her teacher put it. The teacher also said that Barby spent so much time erasing what she had written that she never had time to finish her work at the board.

This mother knew her happy, quiet daughter was just as able as she had been in her first two years of school. To check on it she went over some of Barby's schoolwork with her and found she could handle it all after very simple explanations. Her mother wondered now whether the teacher, whose voice and manner were very positive, might be demanding too much of Barby.

After we talked she made an appointment at school and explained that Barby was shy—like the rest of the family. Then she wondered, out loud, if her daughter wouldn't do better reciting when she chose to, rather than being called on. The teacher got the point, immediately. She said she'd try waiting until Barby raised her hand. She even volunteered to give Barby special assignments to do by herself, then show to the class: maps, illustrations, stories, and so on.

Later my friend told Barby about her talk. She explained that the teacher needed to hear Barby recite in order to find out whether she understood the day's lesson. She tried to encourage her daughter to think of the teacher's goal, rather than worry about the impression she was making. This mother did something else. She made a big point of letting Barbara know that even grown-ups make mistakes; and that mistakes aren't fatal. Barbara helped her make a cake for her aunt's birthday. It came out of the oven flatter than it went in. Barby looked very worried when she saw it, but her mother opened the back door and flipped it into the snow. "The birds will have a party," she said gaily. "Let's try again, shall we?" When Barby's baby brother spilled his milk at supper her mother said, "Get me a towel and sponge, Barby, before the cellar gets flooded. Do you think Adam will learn to eat before he grows up?"

Gradually Barby began to relax about making mistakes. She started to talk in class and let the other children hear some of her very original ideas. She never became the star of third grade, but she started to manage her shyness. And, the next year, with a less awe-inspiring teacher, she gained more self-confidence and could even ask questions when she didn't understand what was going on.

If her mother had concentrated on her failure to get all A's in third grade, Barby might have had a serious setback in adjustment to school, with long-lasting effects.

Children who are restless, curious, "into everything," sometimes become underachievers, too. They don't sit still long enough to get their lessons. Teachers like to call them hyperactive, but they are perfectly normal children and it is no service to them or their parents to pin labels on them. However, they do need attention. The permissive approach, with a teacher who says, "Let

Sally alone; she'll settle down when she gets interested," does not work. It seems to confuse the child and intensify his butterflylike behavior in school. Too severe discipline has almost the same effect. These children need firm, friendly, consistent handling both at school and at home.

Start out with the realistic premise that a very active, restless child is not capable of the same quiet concentration as some other children. Lower your demands. Limit them. Don't expect a restless five-year-old to remember to hang up his clothes, put away his toys, and wash his hands before supper all in one day. When he's having trouble paying attention or being as quiet as the teacher wants in school, let up on your demands at home for a while.

If he's falling behind—or not even starting out in schoolwork, find out from his teacher where he's behind. You and she can do things to help. For example, both the child who can't sit still and the child who can't concentrate for long tend to learn half of what they're supposed to in any one lesson. That means that they're half prepared for the next one. A teacher can help overcome the deficit by taking a little time separately to repeat the part of the lesson the child didn't hear or sit still for. She could keep him after school and make him go through his workbook drill until he finished, but that would be pointless. The work would be all wrong because he would not have heard the lesson it was based on. Far better to find out what he doesn't understand; explain it; see that he understands; then let him do the workbook drill at home—in one or two fifteen-minute periods with his mother or father.

If you can help a child begin to learn in the way that suits him best, you and he both will have some success.

For him this will be the stimulus to further effort, self-control, and more success. He will stay with you, instead of tuning out teachers, parents, and school.

The secret of helping the underachiever is first to give up the idea that every child can or will have the same ambitions for school performance that you have for him. Try to curb your expectations. Make realistic demands. Also, take a candid look at what's going on in the family and in school that might be underneath the lack of interest, attention, enthusiasm, and involvement in learning. Remember that this particular child is not like Timmy, two years older, or Suzy, one year younger. Try to attend to his needs. Figure out how to help him find satisfaction as well as success at home and school. Help him set goals he can meet and then help him meet them. Little by little he will learn to get along with some degree of interest and success.

The most common mistake—and one that is almost unavoidable for some parents—is to panic when you discover that your child is not perfect. Children are so satisfactory to their parents that it comes as an awful shock to learn that other people don't find them quite so marvelous. Don't take it too hard. If you react too strongly, you may end up having to undo the damage caused by your overheated response before you can begin to correct the school problem.

Also, don't immediately accept as gospel everything the experts—whether teacher or psychiatrist—tell you. They can make mistakes as easily as you can, sometimes more easily, before they get acquainted with you and your child. They may also have different standards, values, and goals than you have. Think about what they say. Weigh it all carefully and talk it over at home before you leap to action. Then, if you feel that you must take steps, you are ready to plan and act coolly and sensibly with the child's teacher.

Children with perfectly good brains and no visible behavior problems can be underachievers because they have learning problems. They don't show any signs of them until they start school. Then, despite normal interest, effort, and concentration, they don't make as much progress as they should—especially in reading. You may notice this, even before the teacher discusses it with you. If you try to help, thinking your son or daughter just needs a little encouragement from you, you'll find that the child will forget the simplest words day after day. It's hard to believe he's not putting on an act, trying to be difficult. You may get impatient. It doesn't help. He still won't be able to remember the words you tell him over and over again.

He is not learning because he is not getting the message. There can be any number of reasons. He may not see things the way you or I do. His ability to pay attention is not as well developed for his age as the average child's. He can't relate what he sees on paper—the symbol—to the sound and meaning. He can't connect what he sees with what he writes. There are many learning difficulties (cognitive problems) that make a healthy, intelligent child seem stupid, stubborn, or very lazy to the innocent parent.

I will discuss common learning problems and what to do about them in Chapter 14. I mention them here because I want to alert you to the fact that children who are reasonably intelligent and well adjusted before they start school don't become underachievers because they want to. They are not rebelling, or just being mean. When children's behavior changes suddenly, there's a reason. If you have a perfectly normal, fairly happy, reasonable child who doesn't learn the way you expect, and begins to act tired, bored, moody, or mean, you should find out what's going on right away.

Nowadays most well-trained teachers can pick up signs of learning problems very early in a child's school career. When the symptoms are mild the trouble can usually be corrected with a little extra attention in school. The handicap is overcome before anyone except the teacher knows it's there.

In other cases, expert diagnosis and analysis are needed. If the ordinary teacher or school remedial department can't do what's required, they usually refer parents to a university or private center that administers evaluative tests of intelligence, personality, and learning ability; then recommends remedial treatment.

When you know exactly what is keeping a child from enjoying learning and making progress you and his teachers can help overcome it. You don't run the risk of getting involved in battles of will over schoolwork, punishing your child for something he has no control over, and turning the learning problem into a full-blown social and emotional problem with endless ramifications. Prompt attention helps parents and teachers keep their communication with the child free of static. If you know what is wrong, you aren't likely to act as if the child were stupid, rebellious, or uninterested, and make him want to give up and drop out of school forever.

My mother was a first grade teacher in New York City a good long time ago. When we were little she used to entertain us with stories about "her children." She boasted that no one ever left her classroom without learning to read. She may have exaggerated a bit. We're all entitled to make a good story. But, from what I remember of her methods, it is entirely possible that few children failed her. She never gave them a chance. If children couldn't read, or spell, or write, or add, she didn't call on them. She respected their dignity and worked with them privately while the other children were doing other things. If and when she was sure the child knew one thing, she'd call on him for *that one thing,* so that he had the same sense of achievement and success that the faster children did.

She stayed after school fifteen minutes every day. The children who didn't understand what she was trying to teach in class (today we'd say they had learning lags) sometimes got special help then. Sometimes she'd invite their mothers to come. The mother was never told that her child wasn't doing well. She was simply given specific instructions about how to help him with a particular lesson at home.

When the mother finished her assignment she would let my mother know. Then—and not until then—my mother would call on the child in class, praise him for his good work, and reward him with a penny or a candy and give him a new assignment to take home. All the children got prizes for ability or for effort and in that simpler era when a penny was a treat for a city child, everyone worked hard for them.

When children made mistakes she never scolded. Instead she thanked them for telling her what they didn't know so that she could explain things better. Then she would do a little more teaching until they insisted they understood.

All this made the children she taught relaxed, confident, and secure about themselves. They could ask questions without fear of ridicule, recite when they wanted to, talk up when they simply had something interesting or funny to share. School meant a good time.

The children felt that they were helping my mother teach, and they knew she wanted to help them learn.

No matter how important it seems to you to have your children succeed, you will never—well, almost never—solve their problems by pushing.

This bears infinite repetition: Children want to learn, normally. They keep trying as long as they feel grown-ups are with them. When they see that parents are disappointed and disapproving they begin to give up. If you get involved in school problems, try to keep your mind on the lesson at hand; trust your child's will to please you and his need for your approval, and remember children want to learn as much as you want to see them learn.

11

DIAGNOSTIC FADS

*Labeling Teachers' Problem Children
Doesn't Solve Their Problems*

This year minimal brain dysfunction and hyperactivity
are running neck and neck. Last year perceptual motor
disability was ahead. Before that minimal brain damage
had the lead. Among the psychiatrically oriented,
schizoid tendencies, character defects, lack of motivation, faulty ego structure resulting from depression, or
from a confused family picture, or an overprotective
mother and/or passive father, are current favorites.

There are diagnostic fads among teachers just as there
are dress fads among children—dirty sneakers one season,
loafers with pennies the next.

The only thing is that dress fads are harmless.
Diagnostic fads can be dangerous. They put labels on
children who are not toeing the line their teachers have
set for them. Labels absolve the teacher, but they don't
solve the problem. In fact, labels can make children
problem learners, problems to their parents and problems

to themselves, when initially, the problem may have been the teacher's.

What makes teachers and even principals set themselves up as diagnosticians in such delicate areas as cognitive functioning, neurology, and psychiatry and take it upon themselves to tell parents what's wrong with their children?

For one thing, teachers don't like to admit failure any more than the rest of us do. They can't stand the idea of a child within their reach who is not learning the way children are supposed to, given all the dedication, devotion, and pedagogical expertise they are lavishing upon him. Since teachers don't like to blame themselves when something goes wrong, the natural thing is to blame the child. That was easy in the old days. Everything hinged on moral fiber: "He's lazy." "She is spoiled." "He has to be IT all the time." And so on.

But you can't blame the child any more. Original sin is out of style. Everyone knows children are innocent. There's only one answer—his *problem. Problem,* however, is too vague. It really doesn't say anything. Hence fad diagnoses. Once you give something a name you feel better. No one likes to feel he doesn't know what's wrong.

The children I call BAD GUYS are the ones who usually win the labels.

These are children born with some or all of the following characteristics in various combinations. They move fast. They move a lot. They are easily sidetracked. They don't pay attention very well or very long. They have intense reactions to everything. They have a hard time changing gears: that is, they don't adapt very easily. They don't like to stop what they're doing once they've decided to do it.

Their behavior reflects the temperamental traits they are apparently born with. In our periodic observation of the 231 children included in the New York study of individuality we noticed these behavioral characteristics in the early weeks of life.

These children are very active. They get bored easily. They are restless. If they understand something the first time it is explained, they do not hesitate to let you know that they do not need to hear it again. If they fail to get it the first time, they aren't very happy about listening to it some more. Their attention wanders. They get lost in irrelevant thoughts. They get more restless. They can't contain themselves. They may trip up a friend passing by their desk, or shoot paper clips at a girl across the room to attract attention. They may not accept class routines and schedules very easily. For example, a typical nonadapter gets down to work just when every-one else in the class is about to turn to the next subject. He's the boy who insists on filling in every last one of the pumpkin faces on the page of his workbook instead of getting his reading book out to read with the class. When his classmates started on the workbooks he was busy talking, finding the page, sharpening his pencil, looking out the window, or drawing pictures on the workbook cover.

You can predict that when he finally gets his reading book out he will have to interrupt the class to find out what page to turn to; will need help in finding the place on the page; and will stage a small tantrum if he doesn't get the help he needs finding it.

He's very, very happy when he's happy and very, very cross when he's cross.

If these BAD GUYS are interested and able they are a pleasure to have around. They are so responsive and enthusiastic that they stimulate the rest of the class. Otherwise, they are no fun to teach. If they don't learn easily, they lose interest quickly and fall behind because they do not, cannot, or will not concentrate on what is going on in class long enough to take it in and master it.

They may get labeled whether they learn or not, just because they can be such a nuisance.

There are bad BAD GUYS, and good BAD GUYS. Good BAD GUYS are super-adaptable, super-quiet, super-low-key in their reactions. You might not know they are there. But teachers do. They are dead spots in the room. Dead spots bother teachers almost as much as disruption does. Teachers like to feel that they are getting their message across. The children who speak up, ask questions, give answers, comment, and volunteer to try things and help, reassure them.

When children don't talk much or react much, or otherwise show their eagerness to participate and co-operate, teachers infer that they are not interested, or not paying attention, or are dull. They write them off as blanks until the achievement tests.

If their scores are low, they get labeled: perceptual motor dysfunction, minimal brain dysfunction—or among the psychoanalytically inclined—anxiety neurosis, depressive personality, etc.

Beware the easy label or the snap diagnosis from teachers or other amateurs who are not qualified diagnosticians and have not done the examinations and testing that make reliable diagnosis possible.

In order to help a child learn you have to know what's stopping him. Calling it names does not identify the problem. In fact, the label often becomes an excuse for not teaching children, rather than prescription for helping them learn.

The label may be correct. It may not be. In any case, before you rush off to the nearest psychological testing service or learning expert for confirmation or relief, try the simple home remedy. Look at the child. Look at the teacher. Look at yourself, and see whether anything is wrong with the mix that is keeping your child from getting along in school.

What are the possibilities?

If—in his teacher's mind—he is slow, inattentive, and withdrawn—

Do you find this so at home?

If not, why does he give his teacher this impression?

If he's old enough, ask him. If he says that he's bored, is it because he knows too much? Check! If so, ask the teacher to make him work harder. Is it because he doesn't understand? Check. If so, find out why. Does he say he has no chance to ask questions? See if the teacher can make a point of asking *him* whether he has questions. See if she'll make time during class to investigate for herself whether he has understood new lessons. If he needs more help than she has time for, experiment. See if extra help you can give him will enable him to catch up and keep up.

If you suspect he doesn't ask because he's afraid to, see if more responsibility, less correction, and more praise and more interest in his comments and questions at home will give him more courage at school. Ask the teacher if she will try the same strategy at school and report results.

Take time to check the child's progress yourself, in a casual way. See whether he gets along as steadily and easily as you think he should.

When he asks you questions about homework, do your answers and explanations seem to help him? If

so, go to school and find out firsthand why he is not
learning in class. Perhaps you can see that he is not
getting enough attention and can persuade his teacher
to give him a little extra boost until he catches up.

If you find he is not learning the way you think he
should, at home, ask yourself whether this is a new
development. Has anything happened to trigger it? Is
he worried or upset? Has he been ill? Is he getting enough
sleep? Is he watching too much disturbing TV? Make
any adjustments you think could help.

Or, has your child been a little behind his peers in
some things right along? Was he slow at walking or
talking? Did he take longer than his friends to learn
how to pedal a tricycle? Was he more hesitant to try the
slide and seesaw? If so, he may simply need more time
to get started in school each year—particularly in the first
grades. Wait and watch for a few more weeks.

Your child may be a very bad BAD GUY. His teacher
may say he's hyperactive and suggest pills, or pronounce
minimal brain dysfunction and recommend special education, or just throw up her hands and say help. Again,
examine the situation. Don't panic. Watch the way he
acts at home. Watch the way he plays with other children. Look back over his development and try to review
his progress. Has he become more mature, shown increasing ability to control his impulses, follow instructions, do what you tell him to, take responsibility and
express himself sensibly and clearly? If your answers to
these questions are mostly positive, review the episodes
when his behavior became extreme enough to interfere
with his ability to find out, participate, make friends,
and learn. Are there similar elements in the present
situation that might be triggering the behavior his teacher
is reporting?

Don't assume—because a teacher suggests it—that he is emotionally, neurologically, or mentally impaired. Use your own experience and perceptions about him as the basis for trying to figure out what might be holding him back. Then do what you can at home to help him live more comfortably and get along more effectively. See whether his teacher (once you've shared your views) can make some changes in the classroom that will help him develop the qualities he needs to test what he knows, ask questions, get help when he needs it, and share his ideas and feelings with others.

You cannot expect change overnight. Neither can you anticipate that the super-dynamo, the impulsive, vigorous child, the opinionated, determined nonconformist, or the cool, quiet, retiring, non-participant is ever going to become the typical GOOD GUY who naturally warms the cockles of all teachers' hearts.

On the other hand if you and the child's teacher see no real improvement in his school behavior and work in a matter of months, despite your best joint efforts, I think you will both agree you need further advice. Consult the guidance counselor or your pediatrician about where to turn for diagnosis and treatment.

Your child may end up with the label that his teacher first applied. But with the label, you will have a picture of the psychological, temperamental, emotional, or cognitive difficulties that are handicapping your child, and specific guidance for you and his teacher about how to help the child overcome or cope with them.

12

WORRY OR NOT

*How to Tell a Real Problem from a Passing
Phase, a Bad Day, or the Mirror Image of
Some Anxious Moment of Your Own; and
What to Do*

Worry or not? How can you avoid it when you are all
tied up with someone as close to you and dependent as
a child? Even cool, collected parents are subject to
worry.

You can't expect to rid yourself of worry altogether.
In fact, you shouldn't try to. Worry may be a protective
mechanism, like shyness, that alerts you to danger. But
do try not to overdo it. If you cry wolf too often when
there is no wolf, your child may get to be as anxious
as you are and see himself as a worrisome object with
something seriously wrong.

Here are some common parental worries; signs to
help you sort the true from the false; advice about when
to forget, when to wait, when to act, and what action to
take:

Your six- or seven-year-old is not learning to read
as fast as his classmates.

1. *Don't worry* if he also talked later than your friends' children, but talks normally now. He'll catch up with reading, too. However, do alert his teacher to his past history so she doesn't decide he must be a nonlearner and stop trying to teach him; but, instead, looks for the teaching method that will help him catch up most easily.

2. *Do worry* if he has been quick and able at mastering the other common tasks of growing. Don't just worry. Consult with his teacher. Watch his progress. If he doesn't show some advance during first grade, find out why. If he doesn't read and understand the number work he is being taught in second grade, consult the appropriate specialist and find out the cause.

3. *Do worry* if the teacher's picture of his performance doesn't jibe with your own. Find out whether the school is so strict and repressive that he can't be himself there; or whether he is so unsure of himself and shy that he can't function normally away from home. In either case he needs help.

4. *Do worry* if you have a child who knows the mechanics of reading but doesn't seem to understand the story; knows how to spell but can't use the words he has learned. This may simply be the result of poor teaching, but it could signal a central language problem. If it is, your child might need special remedial work before it interferes with his progress. Talk to his teacher about your concern—if she has not called the problem to your attention. Follow the advice of the school guidance department about getting diagnosis and treatment.

5. *Don't worry* when a child can't explain material or words he has just learned if he can answer your questions about a story after talking about it with you; or use the words he has learned appropriately in conversa-

tion. He probably needs more practice assimilating what he reads; or more careful explanations of assignments than he is getting to make him understand what he is supposed to find out.

Talk to his teacher about what you have observed. She, or the school's special reading teacher, will probably be able to suggest ways to help him master new assignments more efficiently.

6. *Don't worry* when your child takes longer to understand instructions and explanations than his classmates do, as long as he learns in the end. However, make sure that his teachers don't dismiss him as a nonlearner; but understand his style and give him the time and explanation he needs to understand and assimilate new work.

Many normal children catch on slowly—perhaps because we have not yet found the most effective ways to make them learn. Children who take time to grasp new things learn as well as other children. In fact, they may eventually become more profound scholars than some fast learners. If teachers treat them as if they were stupid or slow, of course, they become nonlearners. It is important that they have understanding teachers, and helpful parents.

7. *Don't worry* if your child is a quiet learner who rarely volunteers to answer questions, read his papers to the class, or go to the board. He is probably a happy follower in schoolwork, as in play. As long as he is learning, has friends, and seems contented, there is no reason and little use in trying to change him into a leader.

8. *Don't worry* if your child reverses letters and consonants and numbers quite consistently in first grade. Don't worry if he keeps it up—to a diminishing extent—

in second grade, as long as his basic progress is satisfactory.

9. *Do worry* if a child is making halting progress in reading and is still having trouble getting words and letters in the right order in second grade. Through your teacher, get some expert diagnostic help.

10. *Don't worry* if your child's best friend is ahead of him in reading. Your worry might create a problem (anxiety) where there is none. As long as a child is making progress and feeling good about his work, it doesn't much matter whether he's proceeding at forty or eighty miles an hour. By the time they are ten or eleven most middle class children with normal ability know how to read equally well in terms of speed, skill, and comprehension.

11. *Don't worry* if your child takes twice as long as his teacher expects him to on his homework—getting everything letter perfect and copying over papers until you can't even find an undotted i. Children's ways of doing academic work vary as radically as their taste in clothes. Some don't care what they wear or how, or whether their books and papers are clean or messy. Some thrive on neatness, order, and clarity. There may be no difference at all in their basic performance. Let them alone with their quirks, but

12. *Do worry* if your child is phobic about mistakes and spends so much time getting all work perfect in substance and form that he never gets finished; never really has time to concentrate happily on assimilating and mastering material and making it usable; never enjoys school, because of constant anxiety about how he is doing. Consult his teacher, and, if she suggests, his guidance teacher or a recommended psychologist, or doctor.

13. *Do worry* if your child talks too much; interrupts classmates in spite of repeated correction; asks questions and makes comments that puzzle teachers and children because they don't seem to fit the occasion. Worry, even if his schoolwork is good. He may simply be anxious about his place in the family or the class, because of some relatively unimportant temporary situation. He may have a potentially serious behavioral disturbance. Check his teacher to see what she has observed and what she thinks. If the problem doesn't clear up in a matter of weeks or months, report it to the school guidance specialist or your pediatrician for advice and possibly expert diagnosis.

14. *Do worry* if your child develops tics, new speech problems, or suddenly regresses—acting younger than his years. Typical examples are bed wetting, soiling during the day, baby talk, clinging to parents, wanting to hang on to you in public, avoiding other children—at an age when the child has long since abandoned such behavior in favor of becoming more independent. These are symptoms of conflict and anxiety. Again, consult your school guidance specialist with his teacher; or your own doctor.

15. *Do worry,* too, about destructive behavior. A nursery school child who can't play with other children and doesn't know how to make connections except by knocking over a classmate's block structures, tearing another child's picture, stepping on his doll, or hitting— is having a hard time. Take it seriously—even if school behavior is different from what you see at home. Consult a school guidance counselor or an appropriate specialist to find out what is behind the behavior, and how to deal with it.

16. *Do worry* if your child seems oversensitive to cor-

rection or overwhelmed by failure. A child who is so fearful of making a mistake that he gives up whenever he isn't immediately successful will develop severe learning problems unless he gains the confidence to take chances and persist in the face of failure.

17. *Don't worry* if your teacher complains that your child is too active, noisy, eager to answer, aggressive about showing his classmates how to behave and do their work, as long as he has friends, enjoys himself, and is learning.

18. *Do worry* if he does all the above, and is, in addition, a pain in the neck to you as well as his teacher and classmates, particularly if he is not learning. Consult his teacher and guidance counseler, or your doctor, if the first two don't help. You may find out that you can do things at home that will change your child's school behavior. You may find that emotional or learning problems, needing attention, are the cause of his unpleasant behavior.

19. *Don't worry* about your child because his teacher complains that he is restless and inattentive, if he is learning satisfactorily and getting along with his teacher and friends. Chalk it up to his temperament, but persuade him to try not to interfere with other people's efforts to listen and learn. Co-operate with his teacher's efforts to tone him down a bit.

20. *Do worry* if he is inattentive and not learning, both. Ask his teacher for advice. She might make him more interested in school if she gave him special assignments to keep his attention, called on him more often, and gave him opportunities to move around to relieve his physical restlessness. She might, after a period of close observation, discover that the problem is a learning disability rather than poor behavior.

21. *Don't worry* if a child comes home after one day in first grade and says he'll never go to school again. Don't worry if a child gets suddenly down on school, at any age. Don't even take his complaints seriously unless they persist for some time. Ask what the trouble is, of course. But don't necessarily take the answer at face value.

You might hear a dreadful story from a seven- or even a nine-year-old about how mean the teacher was to a classmate who didn't do a thing wrong, and later learn that the story really concerns your child, who was disciplined for misbehaving. You may hear that your daughter got her pencils stolen when she really lost them. You may hear that the teacher made everyone stay after school for not doing homework when, in fact, your child was the only culprit.

Be sympathetic. Concede that everyone makes mistakes, but remind your child that most teachers try to be fair, most of the time. Try to avoid discussing his threat not to go to school again by suggesting, instead, that he give his teacher another chance.

Recently my grandson returned from his first day in school—which he had eagerly anticipated—saying he hated the teacher and would never go back. His mother found that he had been asked to put his painting away and join the story group. When he didn't respond the teacher asked him to sit by himself. When he cried she told him to cry in the coatroom. He stopped, but he came home dreaming of revenge. If he couldn't do what he wanted, he wouldn't go to school.

His mother didn't argue with him. She said she was sorry he had had a bad time but then she pointed out that since he now knew the class rules he would not need to have any more trouble.

Next day she got him and his older sister ready for

school, talking busily through breakfast. When the bus came he got on, without incident. No more protests.

22. *Do worry* if a child's complaints about school persist and he shows signs of being really unable to get up and go. For example, worry when a child can't get to sleep Sunday nights, week after week. Worry if he can't eat breakfast, or is frequently sick at his stomach after breakfast. Worry if he complains of headaches or sore throats in the morning that go away after the school bus has gone.

These signs don't necessarily suggest deep-seated emotional or learning problems, but they should be checked out. There are many reasons why children don't want to go to school. They may have become victims of a class bully. They may have trouble making friends without mother's customary help. They may be afraid of all strange adults, because of lack of experience. They may not understand what they are supposed to do because the teacher is not observant enough to notice their puzzlement; or because they need more attention than other children. They may be unable to ask for what they need, because of inexperience. They may be lazy or unable to do the necessary preparation or classwork and find staying home the easiest way out. They may have a teacher anyone would try to avoid. They may have heard scare stories about the teacher from teasing neighborhood kids, or older brothers and sisters. They may be having trouble adjusting from a small school to a big impersonal one and just need help learning the ropes and getting used to new responsibility.

It is important to find out whether fears are real or imaginary, so that you can find the way to eliminate them.

In conclusion, parents worry much more than they

need to. They worry so much that they sometimes protect themselves by shoving some of their worries under the covers and trying to ignore them. I may be unusual, but I would advise against this practice. In general, I think it is wiser to face your worries than deny them. An expert can assess your fears objectively. If they are groundless, you can really dismiss them. If they reflect a real problem, it is surely better to discover and treat it than try to worry it away until it may become unmanageable.

WHAT TESTING TELLS

Almost everyone thinks a child's score on the standard intelligence test (his IQ) is an absolute measure of his academic potential. This view both exaggerates and underestimates the significance of the intelligence test.

The IQ does predict a subject's ability, at the moment of testing, to master the standard curriculum of the average American school. It should, since the test is based on standard academic tasks. However, it is a very rough measure of what a child may in fact accomplish, academically, either today or tomorrow.

The temporary state of physical or mental health, temperamental factors, and individual developmental patterns may influence test performance at a given moment and skew a child's score.

Many children perform differently when tests are given en masse to large numbers of children with limited time for explanation and questions. We have found, too, that when small children, particularly those from minority cultural groups, are tested by middle class testers, the scores achieved may be totally unreliable.

But, even under optimum conditions, when a child's score accurately measures his academic potential, circumstances may change his IQ in a matter of years, or even months. Moreover, a variety of factors, including interest; talent; motivation; stimulating, depressing, or frustrating experiences, can make test scores meaningless.

It is almost impossible to predict the influence that temperament, environment, and the subtle combination of things we call motivation can have on children's ability. I remember a brother and sister who would have completely confounded an admissions director relying on test scores. The boy had an IQ just above average—110. His older sister's score was in the very superior range (135). The boy became interested in construction engineering before he got to junior high school. In spite of limited mathematical ability, he passed all the high school math courses with high grades and did well in a demanding engineering school. His sister, with equal encouragement and support from her professional parents, barely finished high school; then dropped out of a second-rate nursing course. She never used her head until she had children—and then only to promote their intellectual development.

It is conceivable that her brother—in spite of the deep interest which gave him the motivation to work hard enough to overachieve—might have been frustrated and turned off completely by indifferent parents, or by a school that measured his potential by his first grade IQ.

Schools, parents, and teachers can have a profound effect—as I have illustrated throughout the book—on whether a child comes to enjoy learning; develops the courage to overcome failure and temporary discouragement; acquires motivating interests; and gets along at somewhere near the intellectual level of which his is capable.

I will never forget a little girl I first met when she

was six. Her IQ was up in the stars, but she was already doing remarkably poorly in the demanding, competitive private school where she was a first-grader. She was totally unsuited for that kind of a school, temperamentally. She was restless, very active, and energetic, very sensitive to other people's reactions and dependent on their approval. All this combined to make it hard for her to pay attention and concentrate on getting her work done, when and if she had understood it. The school required hard work, diligence, independence, initiative, and the self-confidence to withstand almost continuous competitive pressure at work and play.

I advised her parents to transfer her to a school where she would have more opportunity to learn through creative activity—acting out history, for example; re-creating historic times in arts and crafts; learning math with games, etc. She stayed where she was. Her academic career has been a disaster. Schoolwork went from bad to worse and clouded her whole development. She finally went to a third-rate college where she did failing work until she dropped out. So much for that astronomical IQ.

Actually, IQ is only the beginning of what a standard intelligence test can tell us about a child.

The test examines very specific areas of intellectual functioning. Properly administered and evaluated, it can be a powerful tool for getting at the exact cause of learning problems and dictating the most effective treatment.

There are a number of other tests developed in this century that we can use in diagnosis of learning problems.

You don't need to know about even the most important of them. However, since testing is commonly recommended to parents in connection with quite ordinary problems of growing, you might like to know how I use tests to help me decide how to treat children in particular situations.

Learning difficulties come from many different causes: emotional disturbance, generalized defective mental functioning, specific brain damage or dysfunction, an unexplained problem affecting understanding or the ability to communicate, individual temperamental characteristics, defects of hearing or vision, various developmental lags.

By the time I have seen a child once or twice, talked to his parents, gone over his history with them and with his family doctor, and looked at teachers' reports on his academic and social behavior in school, I usually have some ideas about what might be wrong with him. If I am not absolutely certain about the cause of the problem and how to deal with it, I use tests to help clarify my diagnosis.

Let me illustrate with Paul—a nine-year-old boy I have been working with recently. Paul's parents came to me because his schoolwork had been going steadily downhill during the year and his teacher was concerned. She had suggested as tactfully as she could that Paul might be a little "slow," but the parents understood perfectly well that she meant retarded. They had been worried themselves. They had tried to help him at home, at his teacher's suggestion, but, while he seemed painfully eager to learn, their helping was not effective. Besides, they told me, they had noticed that Paul had begun to play with his younger sister's friends, instead of his classmates in the neighborhood.

Paul didn't seem retarded to me. At the end of a couple of visits with him I couldn't believe he *was* retarded.

And I was certainly sure that he was not emotionally disturbed in any way. However, I had no reason to question the parents' report. They were concerned, naturally, but not at all overanxious, or hysterical.

I was puzzled. Slight mental retardation could very easily have gone unnoticed at home. Paul was the first child. His attentive parents were interested and able to show and tell until he understood his world. A teacher could not spend so much time explaining. Possibly in a group, where the pace was geared to the average child, he couldn't get the attention, nor ask for the information he needed to keep up with his peers. In fourth grade, he might be reaching the level where even the effort to keep up was beyond him.

However, I could not shake my conviction that he was normal. If I was correct, how could his decline be explained? Was his attention span shorter than that of most children his age? Was he average in intelligence, but above average in distractibility, so that he never really finished learning any day's lesson? Either of these characteristics would hold him back and either of them could be overlooked by his parents, or by me, or anyone else who could keep Paul's attention by single-minded concentration on him.

Could he have some subtle problem that interfered with his ability to understand or communicate?

These were the questions I had to answer before I could help Paul's parents with their son. I called a psychologist who is an expert in intellectual assessment, talked to her about Paul, then posed my questions.

Orders for psychological testing must be as specific as orders for any diagnostic procedure. If you go to a doctor complaining of a stomach ache he doesn't send you to a laboratory and tell them to test, test, test, without knowing anything about what to look for. Nor do I take out a prescription pad, dash off the word TEST, and tell a patient to deliver it to the psychologist of his choice.

I use a handful of men and women whom I have worked with over the years and found to be skillful and dependable experts, whom children quickly trust. They are good testers and good interpreters. I usually explain all this to parents, and, if they are agreeable, I call one of these testing specialists, discuss the child and his symptoms, and go over the questions I have. With this background, the tester knows what to look for and can best decide what tests and parts of tests are likely to give us the answers we need.

The answers can come from the child's behavior during the tests as well as from the test results. Without the tester's report on any relevant behavior, the results might be misleading. Paul, for example, tested above average in general intelligence, confirming my hunch. However, if I had taken those findings alone, I might have made a serious diagnostic mistake. The tester told me, as well, that she had had trouble keeping his attention during the test. In fact she had spent so much time getting him to put his mind on what he was doing that he took much longer than he should have taken to finish.

I began to find out something about why Paul had trouble keeping up in class. But I still did not understand *why* he could not concentrate better, when he seemed, to his parents and the tester, so interested, willing, and agreeable.

The tester's careful study of the results gave us the essential clue to Paul's problem. She noticed that his scores were uneven. He did perfectly well when it was a question of following single instructions: "Put an X on the wrong answer," for example, or "Divide 96 by 8." When he had to carry out a series of commands, given all at once, he faltered.

He asked for instructions over and over. He spent lots of time chewing his pencil and looking out the window. He kept stretching and wriggling, as if he could not possibly get comfortable. When he finally started to answer the problem his embarrassment at his inadequacy really prevented him from using his head. His performance was way below normal for his age, as a result.

Paul could not remember phone numbers. If you told him to go to the board and write down an arithmetic problem, he would have forgotten it by the time he got there. He had a very specific learning difficulty. His inability to follow any but the simplest oral directions made it impossible for him to learn in the usual classroom. Skilled testing revealed the exact nature of his problem and made it possible for us to work out a tutoring program that helped him concentrate as effectively as he could and learn ways to compensate for his defect.

Testing, as this example shows, not only measures general intelligence, but gives us the raw material we need to locate particular kinds of cognitive disability; estimate how serious it is; how susceptible it might be to treatment; and the kinds of treatment that will work.

A child's behavior during testing tells us a great deal about whether emotional factors are causing or complicating the learning problem.

Rebelliousness, negativism, anxiety, fear, and inattentiveness with emotional roots, will also show up in uneven test scores. A child who is disturbed may score way below normal on measures of certain kinds of thinking, then proceed to stun you by swimming through problems that measure the same kind of thinking at a much higher level.

Tests tell us when learning problems are grounded in individual temperamental characteristics. For example, if a shorter-than-normal attention span is holding a child back, it will show up in tests of basic intellectual skills. The tests are designed so that some of the measures of particular skills require concentration, while others don't. Thus a child who has trouble concentrating will do poorly on the part of the test that takes concentration and well on the part that doesn't.

Certain parts of the intelligence test and other tests, as well, not only suggest, but corroborate or dispel our own hunches about learning problems that stem from inability to understand or to communicate what has been learned.

Unless a child's problem is a very subtle or complicated one, we can usually find out all we need to know about it with the general intelligence test. However, when we want to go further, there are any number of more specialized tests to use: personality tests that allow us to analyze behavioral difficulties; cognitive tests that focus on the nature of learning problems and suggest how to overcome them.

Abuse of intelligence tests—using IQ scores and totally irrelevant IQ differentials as the basis for letting children in, or keeping them out of one school, class, group, or another, has made parents terribly anxious about testing, generally. You should not be. If you have a pediatrician you trust, and a psychologist he trusts, to do the testing, your child will benefit, rather than suffer from testing. When a child has a problem that is getting in his way, your first aim is to solve it as quickly as possible. Testing is often the essential first step. When testing is presented in that light most children—particularly young ones—enjoy the puzzles, games, questions, and tasks involved from beginning to end.

CHAPTER THIRTEEN

Q & A

Q. We want to send our three-year-old daughter to a near-by nursery school. Personality and IQ testing are part of the normal admissions procedure. The school does not take children with IQ's under 120. I once read that children's test scores at this age are meaningless. We are also worried about the effect of the testing on the child.

A. I believe that any experienced observer of young children can tell whether a child is emotionally and mentally able to fit happily into a group of his peers at the nursery school level. Unless the school is in the business of preparing children for a particularly selective elementary school, I can't imagine what use there would be in such testing. However, if you feel the convenience of the school's location and its teachers and program outweigh the inconvenience of having your daughter tested, go ahead. Don't worry about the effects on her. Children at this age enjoy tests as they do any play session with an interested and pleasant grown-up, once they get used to leaving their mothers for a while.

However, I would not take the results very seriously, whether your child makes the grade or not. The scores may reflect how easily she adjusts to strangers and strange situations as much as how smart and mature she is.

Q. In our town children are placed in first grade, according to their IQ scores in spring of kindergarten year. Some parents prepare their children. Is this wise?

A. If you prepare a child for this kind of testing, you do two things that are potentially destructive. First, you make the child anxious about this test and all tests, and betray to him your own concern about how good he is. Once you shake his self-confidence he is *less* prepared rather than better able to settle into school and do well. Second, while the preparation may enable him to get a higher score than he otherwise would, if the score does not truly measure his ability, his secret will be discovered when he is unable to keep up with the group in which he is placed. Then the innocent teacher will think he is not trying and react negatively; and he will feel he is inadequate and suffer. In short, school will be an uncomfortable, nerve-wracking experience from the start, instead of a happy and stimulating one.

Bear in mind that IQ scores can change ten to thirty points up or down, between the ages of three and thirteen. Remember that any child with average intelligence (90 to 110) can learn whatever he needs to know to get along well in adult life, although he probably won't choose scholarship or the professions for a career. The more positive his educational experience is from the beginning, the further he will go. If he likes school, he will try and that will have much more influence on his IQ in the long run than your worrying about test results in kindergarten and grade school.

Q. We took our child to a psychiatrist because he is unhappy about going to school and his teacher reports that he is uncomfortable answering questions in front of his classmates. The psychiatrist recommends testing. How should we prepare our child?

A. Children under nine or ten accept any testing procedure a doctor recommends *if you don't show anxiety.* Take your child to the test as you would for an X ray. Ask the doctor what kinds of tests he has prescribed and what they are like and then explain what they're for to your child. For example, "Your teacher wants us to find out why you are so unhappy in school." Or "We want to help you get along better in school." "The tests may help you find out how to do your work so that you will enjoy learning."

Q. Some friends of ours were told by their thirteen-year-old son's teacher that he had a learning problem and needed expert help. My friends saw an ad for a learning clinic in a near-by town, called for an appointment, and took the boy. The clinic "specialists" tested him, then recommended after-school sessions, three times a week, to help him improve his skills and work habits.

After six months, the boy's marks were much worse. He had changed from pleasant and friendly to sullen and anti-school. Instead of being a quiet nonparticipant in class, he had become a disrupter.

Three thousand dollars of special tutoring later, the boy's doctor referred him to a psychiatrist. He told my friends that the learning clinic is being sued for fraud by the county medical society because its "experts" aren't trained psychologists.

After two sessions the psychiatrist said there was nothing wrong with the boy that a year of growth and a less boring, more sympathetic teacher wouldn't help.

His parents had him switched to a different home

room. He's so happy back with his old after-school social
life that he is almost cheerful already. He's even beginning to respond to the more positive approach of his new
home room teacher.

A. I can't overemphasize the importance of choosing
well-recommended, reputable specialists for diagnosis
and treatment of learning difficulties. Perhaps if your
friends had consulted the school district's guidance
counselor they would have gotten a better steer. Generally, pediatricians will recommend a child psychiatrist
who may do the necessary diagnostic work and testing
himself or refer you to a skilled testing specialist. When
you cannot get guidance and help in this way, ask the
state or county medical society or health department for
advice.

CENTRAL LANGUAGE IMPAIRMENT

Problems with Understanding, Talking, Reading, and Writing: What They Are and What to Do

In many sections of the United States a good-sized minority of school children have trouble learning because English is their second language. But another small group of children (ten to fifteen per cent) have trouble understanding and expressing themselves in any language at all. They have some degree of central language impairment, sometimes called developmental aphasia.

Their problem does not stem from deafness, emotional illness, or mental retardation. In fact they are often unusually bright, attractive, otherwise normal children. For reasons that are still far from clear something is lacking or lagging in the development of the neurological mechanisms that control language function.

Everyone knows that children are all different and that the range in the rate of normal development is very wide. It is probably no more unusual for a child to be slow or uneven in language development than it is for him to be slow in growing or gaining muscular control. However, a lag in language is a lot harder on a first-grader than being small for his age or clumsier than his peers.

Most of us have been talking, reading, and writing, i.e. using language, for so many years that we take our ability to express ourselves and understand others for granted. You can get some idea of the immense difficulty that central language impairment creates for the small child if you have ever seen an adult who has lost all or part of his power to express himself because of an accident to the brain.

When a person has a stroke that affects a part of the brain that governs use of language, he becomes aphasic, i.e. without the use of words.

Sometimes all language function is affected and he forgets how to read, no longer understands what he hears, and cannot speak or write. Frequently, though, only part of his communication system is knocked out, and the healthy areas of the brain that control language take over. When this happens a person, for example, who can no longer speak, may still be able to read, and can thus rebuild his vocabulary with practice and learn to speak again.

When a child is born with developmental aphasia or central language impairment, he is more seriously handicapped. He has no knowledge of language to fall back on for help in overcoming his inability to understand or express himself. Any disturbance affects the development of all of his language functions.

Fortunately, few children are as seriously affected as the aphasic adult. The aphasic child usually has to overcome a lag in a certain aspect of language development. The aphasic adult must learn to compensate for a total absence of function in a certain area. Nevertheless, children with language problems have a hard time. Because they seem smart and otherwise normal, people find it hard to believe that they can't understand plain English or answer properly when spoken to. Their parents think they are being stubborn and contrary and worry about whether they are emotionally disturbed. They may begin to distrust their own judgment and wonder whether the child may not be retarded.

Teachers puzzle over them, too. They'll say: "I can't seem to get through to her." "I know he has something important to tell me, but he just can't seem to express himself." "I can see that he thinks I'm not trying to understand him." "He seems smart, but even when I go over the simplest sounds again and again he doesn't remember them at all."

The children themselves realize something is wrong and, if they are normally intelligent, they begin to find ways to cover up their problem. They pretend they don't hear. They clown around to try to distract attention when they can't give appropriate responses. They often have trouble playing with other children because of their difficulty in communicating, and this adds to their maladjustment. As a result, teachers, too, sometimes make the mistake of thinking they are stupid or emotionally ill.

In the days before aphasia was understood these children were frequently neglected and consigned to oblivion at an early age. The outlook today is much brighter. While very little is known, even now, about the exact cause of developmental language problems, the various forms of central language impairment have been widely enough publicized so that parents and teachers, both, consider aphasia as a possibility when children who start out perfectly normally show signs of having trouble with understanding, speech, reading, or writing.

With early diagnosis and treatment, when it is called for, one child in a thousand will remain seriously handicapped in adult life.

DYSLEXIA is the mildest and by far the most common form of central language impairment. You cannot spot it until children are learning to read. It affects their ability to deal with the printed or written word, only. You can suspect it when children are unusually slow at learning to recognize letters and sounds; write from right to left; and form their letters in mirror fashion.

All children transpose letters to some extent when they start to read. Many mix up letters or combinations, such as b and d, p and q. Such common beginners' mistakes are easy to distinguish from the consistent errors and total inability to remember letters and words that dyslexics demonstrate.

There is a lot of controversy over what dyslexia is and how to handle it. Much that is loosely labeled dyslexia is in reality a temporary lag in language development. It does not require the stringent remedial measures that true dyslexia does.

The child with this transient learning problem should have as much experience as he can get, comfortably and easily, to develop confidence about expressing himself orally. This means experience talking about what he is doing, thinking, seeing, feeling and imagining. It means emphasizing easy expression and not being too fussy about correct pronunciation and sentence structure. Simple, spontaneous, vivid expression is what to aim for.

The distinction between a developmental lag and true dyslexia is hard for the non-professional to make. I would recommend expert diagnosis for any mentally, physically, and emotionally normal child when learning lag persists through the first grade, assuming adequate teaching.

True dyslexia can be mild or quite severe. Some dyslexic children become perfectly comfortable in reading and written expression with time and proper teaching. Some will always have to use compensatory routes for learning and communicating. All dyslexia requires specialized instruction.

Identifying the problem helps clear the atmosphere. Parents and teachers can then stop wondering whether the child is bored, has an emotional block, or is just not trying, and begin to react to him positively. The aim should be to help him stop feeling like a failure or a misfit, drop his defenses and cover-ups, and begin to behave like a normal, happy, curious first- or second-grader.

Dyslexia has no effect on a child's ability to express himself orally, musically, athletically, dramatically, mechanically or artistically. Intelligent and imaginative teachers can help the dyslexic child learn through listening and talking. They can also help by finding ways for him to participate in class work and get recognition for it.

Children can learn a great deal in the years when they are not yet able to read and write. If their school life during that period is happy and interesting, they will be much more willing to work hard to overcome their reading and writing lag, as they become able to, so that the handicap will have a minimal effect on their progress.

I recommend that parents and class-room teachers forget trying to teach reading, writing and spelling to the dyslexic child, temporarily, and concentrate on stimulating his ability to learn and express himself in speech. Remedial work should be carried out in private sessions with a remedial expert, or in special classes for children with similar problems.

Parents play a crucial role. Like teachers, they tend to over-react to the non-reader, because reading is the tool subject on which almost all other learning hinges. They also tend to use a get-tough policy, in reaction to the careless neglect of the non-reader that often occurred with the "They'll-learn-when-they're-ready" approach to reading.

These tactics are invariably self-defeating. They do not solve the dyslexic's problem, and they are so frustrating that they may make the child give up on learning forever.

The best course for parents is to provide the most effective special teaching they can find, and then let the teacher take charge. Accent the positive at home, and avoid the traps: policing homework, nagging for more or better work, and so on.

Specifically: Make sure that the dyslexic child will not have to expose his handicap in the classroom by being forced to participate in regular reading sessions.

Ignore spelling and grammar. Applaud thoughts and ideas when you can, and soft pedal criticism.

Ask the child's regular teacher to do the same if possible.

Ask the teacher to give the child one grade for content and another for spelling and grammar on his written work, if she can.

Symptoms of the other forms of language impairment which usually require treatment are apparent long before children start school. The most obvious signs are late speech, lack of speech, and garbled speech.

Normally, a child says words by the time he is two, and has a vocabulary of at least a half dozen words by the time he is two and a half. If he is not progressing at this level, I would be worried. If he is not talking by three, I would certainly consult an expert without delay. Even if I am not able to make a final diagnosis in a two-and-a-half- or three-year-old, it is very useful to have this early record of his behavior and abilities for comparison when I see how he is getting along, later.

When a child has trouble talking or understanding what people say to him he is inevitably going to have trouble getting along in school. So, the longer his speech problem is left untended, the more risk there is that he will finally have to overcome emotional damage and academic failure in addition to getting over the underlying problem.

As children with language difficulties become more aware of their surroundings they also become more aware of what is wrong with them. Then they develop a full repertory of ways to handle their inability to understand or say what they want to. They act foolish when they can't answer in school, trying to cover up. They may have tantrums over their frustration. They sometimes ignore adults completely—pretending they don't hear. They get into fights with other children because they can't join in the games that are going on. They mess up other children's work because they can't bear to be so left out.

In the bosom of the family, where they are more comfortable, they behave differently. They seem normal so much of the time that parents find it baffling when they act stupid or mean. Mothers and fathers don't know whether to distrust teachers' reports or not. They waver in their own handling of the child. Sometimes—depending on the child's behavior at the time—they are all sympathy and protectiveness, as if the child were mentally or emotionally handicapped. Sometimes they are very tough, responding to what seems sheer orneriness. Parents' confusion is as upsetting to them as it is to the child.

Early diagnosis helps clear the air. A specialist can readily distinguish a language problem from mental retardation or emotional illness. Once parents and teachers know what is wrong, it is much easier for them to work together to help the child.

There are two kinds of serious central language impairment: expressive and receptive.

EXPRESSIVE language impairment is by far the more common. Children who have it understand what they see, hear, and feel, but they cannot always put it into words. They understand what you say to them, but they can't always answer properly.

RECEPTIVE language impairment affects the child's ability to understand what he *hears,* and so this form of language lag also keeps him from expressing himself normally for his age and general level of mental development.

Problems with expression vary in seriousness. Some children are so mildly handicapped that no one notices anything unusual until they start school. Others can be almost speechless, even as old as five.

Perhaps my experiences with some of the children

I know may help you understand the problems, and how they can be overcome.

Nick came to me when he was five years old. His kindergarten teacher thought he was schizophrenic because of his strange, disjointed, circuitous way of expressing himself, and his inappropriate, silly, unpredictable behavior. She said he often babbled instead of answering her questions, clowned, threw tantrums, disrupted other children's play, or went off into what seemed like a world of his own.

He struck me at once as a bright, friendly, direct, independent child for five. He left his mother without any hesitation and lost no time in choosing the toys in the playroom that interested him.

The family had just moved from the country to an apartment in town. Not surprisingly, the game he chose was "moving." He looked on the shelves until he found a moving van and started right in to load it. One of the first things he picked up was a refrigerator.

"What are you packing?" I asked.

He looked at it; looked at me; dropped it quickly; picked up a stove. Then he said, smiling coyly, "It's a stove." No comment from me.

He kept on loading all the furniture and equipment he wanted; drove the van around to an apartment building; then unpacked and arranged the kitchen in his new place. He didn't talk much, except to answer "yes" or "no" to my questions. He started to get dinner. He picked up toy celery.

"I can't see what you're making," I said. "What is it?"

For a second he had the same look of earnest concentration I had noticed when I'd asked about the refrigerator. Then his face clouded over—just for a second.

He recovered, flashed me a big smile, and said, "It's lettuce."

"And what are you going to do with it?" I said, smiling so he knew that I got the joke.

"Put it in the oven," he answered, giggling. Then he started dancing around in a completely disorganized way, throwing the toy food up in the air, feigning hilarity, but being, actually, very upset.

He knew *I* knew it wasn't lettuce and that lettuce doesn't go in ovens. He was putting on an act of exaggerated nonsense to cover up the fact that he could not say "celery" when I asked him a question. He was powerless to cope with his problem or tell me what the trouble was. He understood me, but he couldn't find the right words.

He was like you or me when we have one of those momentary lapses and can't think of the name of a friend we are trying to introduce or a word we know as well as we know our names.

I didn't have to put him through any formal tests. I knew that he was perfectly normal, mentally, if he was smart enough to invent this pretty good deception to cover up his weakness; smart enough to have a very accurate knowledge of categories of objects: lettuce-celery, refrigerator-oven.

I could tell by the way that he left his mother to come with me, and his quick interest in choosing a game and getting started, and his enjoyment of our "togetherness" in the play, that there was nothing at all wrong with him emotionally. He just got stuck on words now and then. The behavior, that—reasonably enough—looked bizarre to his teacher was his way of concealing the fact that he couldn't express himself, when he had so much to say.

I didn't ask any more painful questions. But I played with Nick a little longer just so that he wouldn't go away feeling that I had tricked him into exposing his weakness to me. I asked him to choose what he liked best and he went straight for the puzzles, tipping me off that he could do them well. "I bet you're good at puzzles. Let's get a very hard one." So we picked one together which he proceeded to do with rather spectacular speed, and —needless to say—no help from me. At the end he smiled a real smile. I congratulated him and he ran out to his mother, laughing over his performance.

Nick's problem was not serious. He didn't need any treatment. When his parents realized that he wasn't being mean or stubborn when he gave foolish answers or ignored them, they stopped scolding and teasing him and simply asked again, or waited for him to answer. After his teacher and I talked, she changed her tactics, making things much easier for Nick in school. She avoided putting him on the spot by asking him direct questions in front of the class, and waited for him to volunteer. She arranged for her assistant to play alone with him regularly so that he would have more practice using words.

Nick is now eight. I saw him just last week. He is happy, sociable, and has two good friends who are as adventurous and enthusiastic as he is. He is not the best storyteller in his class, but he is keeping up fairly well and I don't think he will ever have any serious trouble in school. He is going to outgrow his problem.

Janet, a three-year-old I know, is handicapped by receptive language impairment. As I have said, this is less common. It is also much harder to correct. It originates in the part of the brain that decodes language. If a child has trouble figuring out what he hears, then he cannot follow directions or do what he is told. His speech is retarded to the same degree that his understanding of speech is flawed.

When I saw Janet she still couldn't talk well, but she was so normal in every other way that her parents had overlooked her problem. She was happy and cooperative, and loved to help take care of her baby brother—bringing the powder, clean diapers, the pacifier, or the baby food, whenever her mother needed them. It was an aunt who first noticed that Janet did not understand what was *said* to her. She came to take Janet to the zoo in the city, one day. Instead of getting ready when she heard the plan, Janet kept right on playing with the cars she was racing around the living room. Her aunt told her about their excursion again. Janet just looked quizzical. Not until her aunt got Janet's hat and coat out did the child realize what was expected. Then she jumped up, eager to get ready and be off.

Her mother told me about this incident and I asked them to come and see me. When I had spent a half hour with Janet I could see why her parents had missed her problem.

She was bright, observant, responsive, and interested in everything going on around her. By watching carefully, she picked up all the routines of family life and figured out what was expected next—such as bringing her mother a diaper or towel—without having to be told and then understand what was wanted. When the dishes were washed they got dried. When the baby was wet he needed a clean diaper.

We played store—a game which would show me how well Janet understood the world she knew, and how much she could understand when I spoke to her. She was totally absorbed and happy, picking things to buy, paying me, getting change, packing her purchases in her toy shopping cart, and then taking over my role when I gave her a turn.

Her expression was lively and alert except when I asked her a question or made a suggestion. Then she smiled pleasantly and continued her own play until my gestures indicated what I meant.

She was neither stupid nor deaf. She simply did not understand my questions unless she could relate them, by guessing, to the routine of marketing, which she had learned in the course of going shopping with her parents.

There was not a lot that we could do for Janet, except assure her parents that she was normally intelligent. As I had hoped and predicted to them, Janet continued to make progress in communicating as she had already done before I saw her. She was much better able to understand when I saw her at three and a half. Like most normally intelligent children with receptive language defects, she will gradually learn how to compensate for or overcome her difficulty if she gets proper support and guidance.

When she starts school she will probably need to be in a special class for language-impaired children. In these classes there is a great deal of emphasis on speech training with enough trained teachers and aides to see that each child gets many different kinds of opportunities to learn: Games, art, and play are used, as well as more formal drill, to help them connect sounds with letters and meanings. In some cases, children with receptive language problems are able to understand printed and graphic symbols before they can understand words. Therefore early reading drill sometimes hastens their understanding and speech development. We are hopeful that Janet will progress in this way.

Parents always feel guilty when anything is wrong with a child. They can certainly not be blamed for these language problems. Feeling guilty, far from helping, can make things worse. The constructive way to help a language-impaired child is to start, as soon as possible, doing something about correcting his trouble.

CHAPTER FOURTEEN

Q & A

Q. What would make me suspect that my child had a problem in language development (central language impairment)?

A. If your child is a late talker, doesn't talk, or doesn't speak clearly, you should begin comparing him with other children his age, and asking friends and relatives whether they think he is unusual. If a child has almost no vocabulary at two-and-a-half or three, or doesn't seem to understand what you say, you should consult a pediatrician, and/or a specialist in speech development.

Q. How can a nursery school teacher tell when something is wrong?

A. When she sees that a child's speech is much less mature than the rest of his behavior, or that he doesn't seem to react as quickly or intelligently as she would expect from watching him play by himself, or from reading his records and talking to his parents about his behavior at home.

Q. How can I tell a speech problem from mental retardation?

A. If your child seems to act like other children his

age, and learns to do puzzles and card games and follow family routines that don't require him to understand directions, you can be fairly sure he is normally intelligent. Common sense usually tips parents off when they have a retarded child.

Q. How do I know the problem is not emotional?

A. Emotionally healthy youngsters are affectionate, particularly with people they know. Their play reflects their awareness of human relationships and feelings. They use their toys appropriately. For example, they would not pile up cars, trucks, and dolls as if they were blocks.

They ask for help in a natural way. An emotionally ill child, for example, might be playing with cars and get them locked in a collision. If he wanted to get them separated, he might take my hand and put it on the cars, instead of looking at me and telling me by gestures (if he had no words), what he wanted me to do.

Healthy children are usually beginning to be independent at three and can leave their parents to go to school or to play with other children in a house that's familiar. They want to learn to dress themselves and feed themselves and train themselves.

Q. Do parents cause language impairment?

A. This is a problem that we are quite certain parents are not responsible for. We don't know what causes it, but we suspect that it may be hereditary, at least to some extent. Language problems seem to run in families.

I have followed one family of four children. They are all defective in language development except the last. He is only a year old so we cannot tell how he's going to turn out. The three older children all spoke late. They all developed learning problems associated with their difficulty in connecting what they heard (words) with what they saw (letters and words). By the time the third child came along we were prepared. She wasn't as badly handicapped as her older brothers. Besides, her mother was so experienced by then that she started very early playing word, letter, and sound games with her and letting her trace pictures and letters to get the "feel" of sounds. She had no trouble learning to read.

Once I asked the parents if anyone in their families had had speech problems. First, they both said "No." Then the wife reminded her husband—now a Ph.D. in sociology—that she typed his papers for him in graduate school because he was such a poor speller. Bad spelling was the last carry-over from a childhood language problem that had interfered with his progress in elementary school. Like all of us, he had forgotten his problem as fast as he could, once it was behind him.

Q. At what age can children with language problems benefit from treatment?

A. This depends on the child and the severity of the problem. Probably it's a good idea to see what can or needs to be done as soon as you notice that a child is aware of his trouble and suffering from it.

I saw four-year-old Rob a few months ago. He was a perfectly happy child. He was totally silent for the first ten or fifteen minutes we were together. But gradually he warmed up and jabbered away a mile a minute. He talked at exactly the right times. I could tell from the inflection in his voice when he was framing sentences, asking questions, etc., even though I didn't understand a word he was saying. At the end of our session he went out to his father, still talking to me. Then he saw a woman in the waiting room whose face registered shock at his bizarre chatter. He stopped in a flash and didn't say another thing.

Rob was already aware of how strange he sounded. Unless he gets help soon he will have serious social problems created by his fear and self-consciousness.

Q. How will special treatment help if he has to live with people who don't understand him?

A. It won't, unless he can spend a good part of his days with children his own age who have similar problems. Special classes for these children are very important. When they are with children like themselves, who don't think they are "funny" when they talk, they lose their fear and talk more. They learn more because of special teaching and drill. They make more progress because constant practice reinforces their formal training. It's the difference between learning a foreign language at home, or on its native soil. You learn faster when there's no other language to listen to or express yourself in. The environment of a special school gives children more opportunities to learn and more encouragement to try. The congenial setting prevents the emotional problems that come from being misunderstood and isolated.

Recently a guidance teacher in one of the elementary schools that we visited told me about a misbehaving, nonlearning second-grader whom she suspected had a language problem. She persuaded his parents to have him tested. The results convinced everyone that he would be better off in a special school. Now he is ten. He often waits outside his old school to show this guidance teacher his papers and tell her how he is getting along. According to his mother, he is a changed boy. He is doing so well that he will probably be back with his age mates in a regular school in a year or two.

Q. What can parents do at home?

A. Don't attempt any special teaching without instruction from a specialist who has examined the child. Do what trained experts tell you to do—no more, no less. You may find you are simply not temperamentally suited to help. Not everyone has the patience and fortitude required to drill young children—even those who have no handicaps. If you see that you are not succeeding; if you are doing more bargaining, bribing, coaxing, or punishing than teaching, stop.

It would be wiser to find a friendly, tolerant high school or college student who wants experience or money to help your child, and keep your own relationship with him untainted and positive.

Your support and affection are more important than your talents as a drill master.

Q. Is there a risk of being too protective?

A. I don't think so. However, I do think there is a natural tendency to be underdemanding when it is time for the child to assume responsibility for his further progress. When a child has a learning problem, parents are generally told not to push him in the early stages of remedial treatment. That's sound advice. Parents are eager for the child to catch up, for his own sake. But they don't fully appreciate how hard it is to struggle all day with something hard and frustrating; then come home and be asked to start all over. Too much pressure can cause breakdown or explosion.

Once progress has been made, however, practice is necessary in order to maintain the gains. At this point a child may have to shake himself out of his old habits of giving up because he can't, and begin to take responsibility for making headway on his own.

Parents have to steer a narrow course to help. Avoid

letting schoolwork become the focus of family conflict. But try not to be *so* sensitive to the child's difficulties that he never gets the message that *he* has to work to overcome them. Whenever a teacher gives home drill you can be reasonably sure the child is able to do it. Let him know that you expect it to get done.

I remember one mother who handled this well. She had a very strong-minded little boy. Whenever he stopped working she methodically, but firmly and coolly, brought him back to the subject. The teacher sent home assignments for his mother to work on with him. When one was mastered she would notify the teacher, who then sent home another. Jeff invariably left it in his desk. This would go on for a couple of days. He would find excuses. He had promised Billy, next door, to play. After he played he was "too tired." And so on. This mother was tolerant to a point. On day number four she clamped down. The time to work was then and there. No more excuses. Jeff would cry and struggle. When he finished they'd start work. In ten minutes—because she was cool and firm and made it as interesting as possible—he'd become so absorbed he didn't want to stop. She was just as firm about stopping as she was about getting started in the first place. When he learned the words she'd set down for the day's work, that was all. She knew his capacity and always stopped while he was going strong, on the theory that it would be easier to get him started the next day.

Q. How do you decide whether to start remedial work?

A. You must pay attention to the child as well as to his problem. The nature and seriousness of the problem, the temperament of the child, his adjustment at home and at school, his interest in learning are the factors that

I consider in advising parents to wait and see, or to begin treatment.

Some children develop their own ways of handling their language problem until it finally is outgrown. I remember an eight-year-old who told me that his brother took him for a special treat to a bar. As soon as he said it he knew he had the wrong word. "No, it couldn't have been a bar. It was like a bar, but we had a different drink." He described an ice cream soda. I filled in, "Was it an ice cream parlor?" Of course it was. This child was using his good intelligence to help him over his stumbling block. In an understanding and patient family and in a school where classes are small he'd find his own way out of his problem. In fact he might do better than he would if we tried to introduce new methods to him.

It reminds me of the shifting fashions in handling left-handed children. First they were made to learn to write with their "wrong" hand. Later they were encouraged to write with their natural writing hand. Then, as child-centered education spread, they were sometimes "helped" to write with their left hands, without writing upside down in the cramped manner that looks so painful to others and smudges everything they write besides.

Most "lefties" could learn to write "rightie." They could manage, uncomfortably or not, to write left-handed. The only thing that drove them up the wall was the scientific, easier way to improve their left-handed style. They simply could not shift from the way they had taught themselves. So, with children who have slight language problems. If they have found their own way over their stumbling block, it is probably the best way for them.

Children are usually their own best teachers, given the essential foundation. And, as long as they are unafraid, they will let you know when they need help.

GUIDANCE TEACHERS

What They Are; How to Use Them

A few weeks ago I was waiting to see a guidance teacher in a large city school about one of the children in our New York study. I had made an appointment, of course, but it didn't matter. So many children were waiting to see her when I arrived that there was no way she could keep up with her schedule. Since she did not even have the privacy of a separate office, I heard and saw everything that went on, while I was waiting.

Each child handed her a slip, without speaking. Then, without any introductory pleasantries, she started off, "I see you're disturbing the class. Why do you do that?"

The child would mutter an excuse: "My friend asked me a question."

The guidance teacher flipped through the child's file. "You and your friend seem to have lots of questions. Why don't you ask after class?" Then, without waiting for an answer, she said, "I don't want to have to see you here again."

The child got up and left. The next child sat down. The incident repeated itself, again and again.

Perhaps the guidance teacher could have done better. But it is hard to imagine how. She is one person in a school for one thousand city children, who have more than their share of problems. She is getting every one of them from incompetent or helpless teachers who refer the child who chews gum in class and the child who is in urgent need of psychiatric help indiscriminately.

There are just not minutes enough in her day to sort out the minor disciplinary problems that teachers ordinarily can handle themselves from the problems of academic performance or social behavior that signal teachers and parents to take notice, initiate some kind of supportive steps, or get immediate expert advice.

She was acting primarily as a safety valve to give teachers momentary relief from any kind of worrying or troublesome distraction in the classroom.

This is not what a guidance teacher should be doing. When her work is reduced to clerical, pseudo-police duty, the office is misused, abused, and wasted.

Parents need to know what guidance teachers are for in order to judge whether the one in their child's school is a dependable aide to turn to in time of doubt or need.

The guidance teacher's role differs from the elementary school to the junior high and high school level. Lower school guidance teachers rarely do school counseling, other than helping parents find appropriate schools, treatment centers, or remedial clinics for children with special needs that the public school cannot meet. However, in the upper grades, one of the guidance teacher's more important functions is vocational school and college counseling and placement.

Guidance teachers at all school levels should offer

unique insights to parents and teachers about children. They usually have a background of classroom teaching at the age level they are serving, and therefore have a perspective that parents, teachers, and specialists cannot have. They know, firsthand, how a child's behavior affects his adjustment and performance in the classroom; how it affects the teacher's ability to teach, and thus, her attitude toward the child. They can judge when a classroom cannot accommodate a child with a particular problem; how successful various adjustments in handling him, or specific remedial measures may be; and probably can tell, almost instinctively, when to call for help.

Besides the valuable firsthand experience that enables the guidance teacher to offer ideas about manipulating the situation at school or at home to help the parent and child, she should have training in child development, psychology, and learning problems.

She should be able to talk to children and gain their confidence; assess their strengths and weaknesses; detect behavioral, developmental, and learning problems; investigate suspected ones and know when to get more experienced diagnostic advice.

What, specifically, can you expect from a guidance teacher in the elementary grades?

Teachers use them for advice about difficult classroom situations that may involve several children; or for advice about handling individual children with problems, or children who are problems to their teachers.

They may ask a guidance teacher's opinion about a child before talking to parents. Teachers and parents, together, might get advice about a child's work, so that they can develop a joint plan for helping him get along better in school.

Parents, on their own, might ask a guidance teacher for advice when they feel their child would do better in another class. The guidance teacher is the person they turn to when trying to decide whether a child's problems are serious enough to warrant outside consultation. Parents should feel confident in a qualified guidance teacher's judgment in such a situation.

The guidance teacher should not be pro-school, pro-teacher, or pro-parent. The guidance teacher should be the child's advocate, trying to see him as objectively as possible and acting to promote his best development. Far from being the disciplinarian or the gate through which all children who bother teachers must pass before getting back to class, the guidance teacher should be the person from whom children can expect understanding, interest, and support; and to whom they can turn, on their own, in troubling situations, for sympathetic listening, wise advice, and faithful support.

A really good guidance teacher who is not over-worked should also do some preventive work with children. If she keeps her eyes and ears open, she can often help a child before teachers or parents know help is needed.

For example, a guidance teacher noticed that an eight-year-old named Sally passed her office at the same time every Wednesday on her way to the school nurse next door. After a lot of Wednesdays she asked the nurse what Sally came for and found she had a Wednesday-morning stomach ache that always disappeared in half an hour. The guidance teacher asked Sally's teacher what happened Wednesday morning at ten-thirty in class 3-3, and found that was the weekly period for children to make speeches, recite, sing, dance, or otherwise entertain the class. It was just too much for Sally. At her guidance teacher's suggestion Sally's teacher stopped asking her to perform. Instead she helped Sally pick out a poem or famous speech to read to her classmates every week. Sally's stomach aches stopped abruptly. Two months later when the guidance teacher made a check, she found that Sally had so completely forgotten her panic at performing that she was now writing and reciting her own poems on Wednesday mornings.

I once treated a child for a developmental-learning lag that had already made her fall very far behind her third grade classmates. After she began to get special remedial help she improved very quickly. By the end of the school year she was perfectly capable of keeping up with her classmates. However, she got very nervous about going to school the next fall. Her teacher told me that she could barely bring herself to read out loud in front of her classmates, and was also having trouble doing her individual work. I asked the guidance teacher to step in. She was marvelous. First she observed my patient in different classes for several days. Then she spent some time with Barbara until the child felt confident enough to tell about her fears of being made fun of for mistakes. This was the cue the guidance teacher needed. After that she managed to find time to go over each day's reading with Barbara before class until Barbara was sure of herself. After a few weeks of this special support the child asked timidly whether she could stop coming. Needless to say the guidance teacher excused her immediately.

Just recently an old friend of mine told me her eleven-year-old was in trouble with his teacher. According to her, Ned was often late; took longer than necessary to get the late slip signed so he could come into class; seemed to be making an unusual number of trips to the bathroom each day; got into so much classroom mischief that he was sent to the principal's office regularly.

While Ned had never been a very good student, he had never been a disruptive one. I called on the guidance teacher to investigate. She gave me the answer in a few days, after watching Ned in class and testing his knowledge of fifth grade work. Ned had suddenly discovered that his imperfect mastery of reading and math skills had caught up with him. He was unable to do the amount of reading and math required in fifth grade fast enough to finish tests. Midterms were coming up and he knew he was going to fail. Instead of working harder and spending more time on his homework, he had given up. Coming late and misbehaving in class were the ploys he used to avoid exposing his inadequacy altogether.

His parents ran a pretty strict household. They gave Ned his choice of special tutoring, three afternoons a week, plus Saturday morning (when his football team played), or switching to a tutoring school until he caught up. He couldn't face being separated from his friends so he chose to miss the football season and submitted to the special drill.

Another guidance teacher did preliminary testing that uncovered a very obscure learning disability in another child who became a patient of mine.

Guidance teachers have been extremely helpful in finding the proper kind of college or vocational training for some of the children I have worked with. One boy had had a miserable time in school right through from first grade. Very severe dyslexia made learning really painful. With an awful lot of drill and remedial help he had finally made it. He was in the last year of high school. Whenever I saw him he boasted—a little too much,

I thought—about his interest and skill in electronics and photography.

I wasn't really qualified to judge how good he was, but I wanted him to enjoy school for a change. I recommended a school of photography. His guidance teacher knew my patient better than I did. She told me that he didn't want to go to a straight photography school, right away, because he was afraid of not being good enough and being a failure once more. She found a liberal arts college with rather free academic requirements and a very good film-making and photography department. She took care of interpreting the boy's special difficulties to the college and making sure that allowance could be made. She made sure that the college could provide the proper training in technical photographic skills so he would be eligible for good jobs in photography, even if he did not become a superior photographer.

The boy is now in his second year and so happy and involved I can hardly recognize him. Besides, according to the people he's worked for during the summer, he *is* good.

How can you use a guidance teacher most effectively?

Get to know her before you need her. Make sure that she knows your child. Under ideal circumstances, guidance teachers should get acquainted with each child soon after he enters school and have opportunities each year to see him and see how he is getting along and developing. This helps the guidance person detect incipient problems and gives her a reference for judging what changes have taken place, when and if trouble occurs.

When children cannot get along with a particular teacher, don't hesitate to present the problem to the guidance teacher. It is not unusual for a perfectly fine teacher to have trouble with a perfectly fine child. No one is congenial with everyone he runs into, and teachers and children are no exception. The guidance teacher is in a position to judge whether the strange case of incompatibility is serious enough to warrant changing the child to another class and teacher. She can advise you how to help the child and the teacher work together more constructively, if she thinks this is a possibility.

She should also be able to tell you when the child's problems with the teacher are imagined; in which case she might advise you about helping the child see his teacher in a more sympathetic light and develop more trust in her good intentions toward him.

When and if a guidance teacher reports a problem, trust her judgment, unless you have substantial reason not to. It is a good deal better to investigate a problem when it is pointed out, even if it proves to be insignificant, than to disregard warning signals. Teachers and guidance teachers are not apt to be alarmists. They usually err on the side of waiting too long.

On the other hand, don't look for problems. I find there are almost as many parents who insist on problems that teachers and guidance teachers can't find, as there are persons who refuse to admit problems that are staring them in the face. Trust the guidance teacher's judgment.

I know a woman whose two children are five years apart. When the older child was very little this mother had two periods of severe mental illness. Once or twice she was taken to the hospital in the middle of the night and had to be away for weeks at a time. When the older daughter, Linda, started school, she was very shy and quiet. Her mother naturally began worrying about the effect of her illness on the child. I saw Linda several times during first grade. Every time she came to my office she seemed more self-assured. She expressed herself better, played more freely, and seemed to be more spontaneous and comfortable with me.

Nevertheless, her mother could not believe that she was developing normally. In the beginning of second grade she consulted the school guidance teacher, who also made a very thorough check, concluding that Linda was just fine. Her mother remains unconvinced.

I find many parents have a kind of underlying anxiety about their children that is very hard to relieve. Children pick up this kind of chronically anxious attitude from their parents. When you have been assured by teachers and guidance teachers that your children are getting along satisfactorily, try to relax and enjoy life with them, instead of burdening them with your apprehensions.

On the other hand, if there is an acknowledged problem, try to co-operate as fully as you can with school efforts to solve it. Understandably, parents have some hesitation about letting the family skeletons out of the closet. There is no reason why you should confide your private business or personal concerns either to teachers or guidance personnel. Recognize, however, that there are family situations that have such important bearing on children's development and behavior that no guidance teacher or private consultant can possibly help without having some background about what is going on. You don't need to tell all. It is usually enough to report that the child may be reacting to a difficult and upsetting family situation—temporary or chronic.

A number of years ago some friends of ours were practically ostracized in the small town where they lived, because they stood up for their principles during a period of national hysteria. The situation became so untenable for parents and children that they moved to a large city where they could live more anonymously. The children started a new school and everything seemed fine at first. Then Paul, the middle child, who was just thirteen, began to get terrible conduct reports. He had always been a good student. He had never had trouble with children or teachers before. Now, his teacher reported, he was sullen, unfriendly, critical of all his classmates' contributions in the classroom or at gym. In short, he was fast becoming the class enemy. The school recommended psychiatric help. We talked about it. I was sure Paul didn't need psychiatric help at all and would recover his equilibrium as soon as he got over the unpleasant experience he had been through. In the meantime his teacher would have to handle him with kid gloves and she wouldn't be inspired to do that unless she knew that he was not his *normal* self. His parents couldn't face talking to the guidance teacher about their problem. Paul kept getting worse.

Finally I persuaded my friends to tell the guidance teacher—without going into any detail—that the family had been through a very painful period; and to ask for special indulgence for Paul until he recovered. The guidance teacher was immediately helpful. Paul's teacher ignored as much of his bad behavior as possible and looked for opportunities to encourage him to join class discussions, where he excelled. His enthusiasm for school began to revive, as a result, and by the end of the year the chip was off his shoulder and he was his old self again.

The quality of a school's vocational and college advice is so important that I would do some checking before depending on it exclusively. Advisers should be very familiar with the resources of the community or region in which you live. They should have a good general knowledge of the kinds of opportunities that are currently available elsewhere. They should take the time to examine closely each child's abilities, aptitudes, and interests; and they should be able to inspire students to confide their hopes and fears and interests in study and work.

All too often the guidance teacher goes down the list of juniors or seniors, schedules interviews with each child; asks him whether he wants to go to college; asks where he wants to go; sends him to the nearest trade school if he rejects college and that's that.

A good adviser will talk to parents and child together and have at least one session with the child alone. If the child has very definite interests—vocational or professional—that he wants to follow, advising is easy. The counselor offers the catalogues of the schools or colleges that give the training desired, points out the requirements for each school, and estimates the child's chances for acceptance. After visits to the favored schools, which she often arranges, she finally helps with applications and records for the two or three schools of the child's choice.

Most high school juniors have little or no idea of what they want to do next. The guidance teacher's role in these cases is much more subtle. She wants to steer the child to further education and training that will interest him, without shutting off career options prematurely. If a student says he's through with school and never wants to see a book again, she should know something about him and his record before she takes him at his word and ships him off to the plumbers' apprentice program. If he says he wouldn't consider college, he likes cars, she should take the time and have the interest to talk a bit about other opportunities in the field of mechanics, and get him to consider whether he wants to become a toolmaker, for example, with the various fringe benefits and salary bonuses that go with it, or apprentice himself to a local garageman to become a straight mechanic.

If a student wants vocational training, she should be able to point out the advantages of private schools over city or state institutions; the advantages of starting at a near-by community college; the advantages of apprenticeship over classroom training; and so on.

She should be able to offer up-to-date information on colleges, curricula, admissions standards. She should know the strong and weak departments at important schools, and be able to point out innovative programs. She should know each child well enough to be able to make a good and satisfying match for him with a college of his choice.

If you don't trust your school's college advisory service, there are several alternatives. Do it yourself—with the help of advice and information from a magazine or newspaper that has a college and school information department. Or ask your high school principal, or friends who have had children in college, for names of reputable commercial advisory services in your area. Your school or town library may suggest recent editions of school and college directories that will give you some preliminary ideas about places to investigate.

In spite of its strategic importance to school children from first grade to college entrance, guidance is still considered a frill in many quarters. The guidance teacher is looked on often, even by the rest of the faculty, as a kind of psychiatry nut who thinks understanding can take the place of the tough-minded discipline that *they* feel most kids need to straighten out and get in line.

As a result, guidance is not very often what it should be. Children are pushed aside while the guidance teacher is overloaded with requests to sign slips, read doctors' excuses, process children expelled from class for minor infringements, and so on. In this atmosphere the guidance teacher becomes the tool for getting rid of children with adjustment or learning problems that good guidance could help.

Children who don't believe or don't learn are pinned with the popular tags—hyperactivity, minimal brain dysfunction—and referred to special schools which they may not need at all.

School guidance should be considered an essential service to the families of the community. If the parents in your school agree that your guidance service is inadequate, you may be able to find help at private counseling centers or from your own doctor. However, the children who may need guidance the most often have no such alternative. Promoting a competent, well-staffed guidance department in your public schools is one of the most valuable programs a parents' association could undertake.

THE PROS AND CONS OF DAY CARE

Thirty years ago a mother who put her child in nursery school before the age of three was frowned on by the experts. Many nursery school teachers had a kind of missionary zeal. They went about their work trying to make up to their small charges for the ill effects of their "rejecting" mothers.

Even ten years ago most child development specialists believed that separation from the mother figure (and none thought of Daddy, Aunty, or the family nurse in that connection) before three was VERY traumatic. Trauma would show up in shallow emotional responses, apathy, inability to love or learn, and a tendency to deep depression.

Now the pendulum has swung so violently that we may soon be advising parents to put their infants in day care shortly after they get home from the hospital.

I think this is a healthy reversal, all told, for mothers, fathers, and children, too. The ideal family in the ideal family home—father happily at work; mother at home creating a secure, comfortable, stimulating, understanding, consistent physical and emotional environment for children—has long been more dream than reality.

The middle class family has moved from Main Street

—next door to parents, aunts, uncles, cousins, and life-long friends.

Instead of the friendly neighborhood where everyone kept an eye out, and even toddlers were free to explore their turf from breakfast to bedtime with very brief time out for meals, Mommy, Daddy, and baby (if the family is whole) live all alone in a three- or four-room apartment in the city with thirty to several hundred unknown neighbors, all alone, too, or, almost equally isolated from neighbors, in the suburbs.

Daddy's main object is to make enough to get a bigger home, a car, a country place. Mommy's job is to keep busy with very little to occupy her except baby. The almost inevitable result for the baby is too little room to play in, too little freedom *in* play, and too much attention from Mommy.

For Mommy, it's too much investment in baby, producing too much pressure on Daddy to produce the money to provide the escape.

Day care opens the options. It allows women to work *and* have children. Even when the job is not utopia, it adds to the family income and gives a woman companionship with people her own age. It also has bonuses for baby. It gives *him* people *his* own age, and at least an approximation of the space, equipment, materials, and casual but concerned supervision he might once have enjoyed when ideal families lived in ideal towns.

More and more middle class mothers are going back to work.

Another group of women who are not living the American dream life we like to imagine prevails are women who, because of separation, divorce, death, or abandonment, are heads of families. Many of them are poor, living on welfare.

They may be the best, most loving mothers on earth, but circumstances get in their way. Most of them are apartment-bound, most of the time, taking care of babies. Their toddlers are shut in with them—no place to play; no one to play with; TV for toys and companionship. The isolation and emptiness are as bad for mothers as they are for children.

Day care gives women on welfare, who want it, a chance to go back to school to get job training, to go to work. It makes life livable and independence imaginable. It can give their children a civilized childhood.

The question is, can day care really meet the needs of very young children?

Fiorello H. La Guardia, mayor of New York in the mythical thirties and forties, used to say that the worst mother was better than the best day care.

This was good politics. Since, to recoin his phrase, the worst mother is cheaper than the best day care, it was good for the budget. It also won votes—male *and* female —in that era when mother's place was almost uncontestedly in the home.

Politics aside, however, La Guardia's view was the enlightened view at that time. Experts in child development believed that healthy personality growth depends on a close and continuing relationship in the early years with the first person in life—the mother who saves the newborn infant from the initial terror of hunger.

Studies available at the time supported the belief that separation during the first three years when the child is establishing his sense of himself—his identity—seriously cripples his personality for good. It seemed to the experts who observed children in institutions and studied adults who had spent these critical years in children's homes, that children, taken away from their mothers, never really get over the loss. Deprived of the only relationship they know while still incapable of making others, they suffer a permanent decline. They are never able to make friends, form stable, close relationships with either sex, or develop deep interests and commitment to work.

By the sixties, students of child development were a lot less willing to accept such arbitrary pronouncements. They had seen children from so-called happy families develop the personality problems attributed to separation, and they had seen others grow up hale and hardy in institutions. They suspected that there was more to healthy growth than being close to mother.

One of the most sensational clues came from looking up a group of people who had been brought up in an old folks' home. As children, they had been removed from an orphanage to relieve overcrowding there, and more or less unceremoniously deposited in a home for the aged. Ironically, they were selected because they were considered retarded and therefore, presumably, had nothing to lose.

Years later, a psychology graduate student heard about this episode and decided to find out what happened to the children. Much to his initial surprise, he found them normally intelligent, leading normal, satisfactory lives, while many of the favored peers they had left behind carried the scars usually attributed to early separation from mother.

He found the explanation for this unlikely development in the stories the study group told of their childhoods in the home. The lonely old people had embraced them as their own. Their fond, attentive care had literally made the orphans whole. The children who stayed behind, on the other hand, suffered the effects of the scientifically hygienic but emotionally sterile care that prevailed in children's institutions at the time.

It is not so much loss of mother, but lack of adequate mothering, whether inside or outside of institutions, that interferes with healthy personality development.

What every child needs is someone dependable who understands just who he is and knows how to do what's best for him. This may be his mother and father or nurse, or the seventeen-year-old aide with a high school diploma in the day care center he goes to—singly or all together.

Dependable, responsive care is what makes little children become conscious of their own physical and emotional natures; comfortable with themselves as they are; trusting enough to give and receive love; and gradually able to take their places as active, interested members of the human race.

It was this kind of loving attention from the lonely men and women in the old people's home that saved the "retarded" orphans, and it is the kind of care you should look for, first and foremost, when you select a day care center for your child.

Later in this chapter I will list all the requirements I think a good day care center should have. But first, I would like to create for you the atmosphere that should prevail in a good center, by recalling a scene from my days as a young psychiatrist. One of my jobs was to supervise the social workers in a fledgling day nursery operating on the proverbial shoestring in central Harlem.

My students came to the hospital to report to me, but I began to want to see the teachers, the parents, and children and the place where they spent their days, through my own eyes. I paid the center a visit, thinking it would be my first and last, but the center and its staff taught me so much about how to deal with mothers and children that I went back often.

This day nursery would not have won any stars for cleanliness, cheery decoration, or up-to-the-minute equipment, but it felt like home. Not any old home, but the one we all wish we had come from. The coffee was always ready to pour for a parent who might want to stop and talk, and someone was ready to listen, and offer information and advice when asked. The children who were old enough to walk and talk came in—more often than not—bursting with some important information to tell a particular teacher or helper, *right away*. The teacher looked at each child and listened. Often she would touch the child, too, in that casually attentive way parents have; tucking a stray lock into a barrette, retying a shoe, just taking a hand, or stroking a head.

As early as 6 A.M. mothers started bringing their sleepy babies and toddlers. Each teacher would take her particular charges and put them back to sleep for as long as they liked. There were enough teachers and helpers (not as well trained, but no less interested) to give the children the individual attention that a good mother gives, according to her child's individual needs.

Mothers were never pushed aside. No matter what time of day or night it was when they came, there was always someone there to see if there was anything they wanted to ask or tell, and to report the children's latest feats.

You could tell by the number of parents who stopped to chat that they felt welcome; that it was easy for them to keep in touch with their children's progress from day to day.

The director was more than well trained. She had a natural talent with people. She could teach without dictating, and correct without belittling. The younger workers followed her footsteps in spontaneous reaction to her interest, and the effectiveness of her methods.

There was sensible physical care, as there was concern for children's feelings. There was a place to isolate sick ones and someone to keep an eye on them.

There was enough equipment to allow the usual round of play—a housekeeping corner with dolls, dishes, sink, stove, and furniture, blocks and space to build in, a sandbox, a phonograph, storybooks, dress-up clothes, paints, paper, brushes, crayons, paste and scissors, things to climb and things to crawl through, and, of course, wagons and tricycles.

There was a style and structure, so that children could feel something around them from which to take their bearings. For example, in a matter of an hour or so I could figure out the rules: no hitting, or biting; solve your differences if you can, by talking, and when you can't, we'll help you; take turns, but learn to defend your rights.

The helpers did not hover. The children played by themselves. But they did not get too deep into hitting, kicking, hair-pulling, biting fights. With help at the beginning, they gradually learned to solve things themselves as they got to be three and four years old. The shy gradually mustered the confidence to assert themselves. The clinging, difficult ones got comfort, but also guidance, so they learned in the end to enjoy group activity, and to make good friends.

Snacktimes and mealtimes were formal, to a point. Teachers, children, and helpers all sat together. The children learned to serve and pour and pass and carried on lively conversations about their families and their experiences and their work in the center.

The center had an informal academic curriculum every bit as purposeful as any fifth grade's. The day included the usual round of quiet play (dolls, sandbox, blocks, water play, art, music) and active play (dancing, singing, climbing, crawling, riding).

By questioning and experimenting, looking and listening, the children learned the meaning of words, concepts, and colors. They learned to associate pictures and sounds, letters and sounds, and finally, words and sounds. In short, without anyone trying to teach them, forcibly, they got the proper foundation for reading. There were many ways, from making applesauce to buying food for a park trip, that taught them numbers and sizes and many other things about their world and how it works and the fun of finding out.

A lot of nonacademic learning took place, too. Older children already knew about turns. "Can I have that red one after you?" "Are you nearly ready to get off the tricycle?" I heard over and over. The bigger children often noticed when a smaller child was unhappy, and they comforted him. They all showed the trust that comes from being well cared for.

The first day I came I sat quietly to watch until I got oriented. I felt a foot in my lap. There was a little girl smiling up at me with big black eyes. "Please?" She was perfectly confident from past experience that grown-ups help you, and that this particular one would tie her shoe.

A few minutes later a little boy came up with a book. "Read me," he said, sliding confidently onto my lap.

This unpretentious day care center with its gentle staff, chosen and inspired by a devoted and able director, managed almost unfailingly to give its children a warm, comfortable, yet stimulating home by day.

It was remarkable. It would be remarkable now.

What I have seen firsthand, and what specialists tell me, indicate that you will have a hard time finding a place for your child in a center of this quality. The child-caring agencies of our government have never planned or provided realistically for the public care of preschool children. The exploding need and demand for day care during the past decade has changed nothing. In fact the present Administration has cut the funds and tightened the eligibility requirements for federally funded day care.

The result, as you might predict, is chaos: a rag-bag assortment of group care programs—family, commercial, voluntary, and public, with and without government funding. Licensing provisions are more honored in the breach than the observance. As one official said, "You think twice about closing up a substandard center when you don't know what the alternative might be for the children. As long as they are not being maltreated we look the other way."

There is only one training program for day care workers and supervisors in New York City, but even untrained workers are hard to attract, let alone hold. Because you need almost no credentials, the pay is low, and the future precarious, day care attracts young people who drift in and out between here and there, about as concerned with children and program as they would be with dishwashing, or any other pickup job you can get when you are untrained and on the move.

Here is the scene in one twenty-four-hour center with three hundred children—aged two months to four years—enrolled. Take the infants. There are twenty-five of them under a year old in a dark, drafty, unpainted room below street level, opening directly onto a noisy city street. Three or four blank-faced attendants look on limply.

Some babies sleep in their net-walled playpens lined "bumper-to-bumper" around the wall—shoes on, clothes on. Some sit crying. Some sit. An efficient matron-figure changes a baby now and then, picking it up and plunking it down like a bag of flour, without talking, or looking. There is one old rubber ball. The matron occasionally rolls it absently at a crying baby. The glum-faced attendants crack their gum and look into space. A baby crawls to me, apparently seeing some response in my eye. I say nothing. It pulls itself up against my leg and reaches for my hand. I have to respond. The matron-figure swoops down and takes the baby away, saying, "No, no." The baby, a persistent child, tries again; is again restrained; then lies down on the floor and cries softly.

A baby wakes up; is silently changed; washed with the same cloth used for others; plunked down. It cries for a while and then sits—eyes running, nose running, sad and forlorn. I ask the child's name. No one knows. I ask the age. The matron says, "I'd have to see the chart." I ask the workers how long they've been there. One of the four had been with the babies for three weeks. The rest for a week or two.

I have been assured that there is not another center like this anywhere in the country. Nevertheless, if you want good day care, I would plan for it before I planned a child. I imagine you might find space in a good center if you applied at the time of your confirming visit to your obstetrician. I would suggest investigating the possibility of family care—where one woman cares for three or four babies of approximately the same age—as well as looking at established day care centers.

Universal day care is essential if we are to solve the central problems that men, women, and children face today. But day care is no cure-all. If parents see it as a panacea, enrolling babies and toddlers in the nearest center as routinely as they put their five-year-olds in kindergarten, the general level of day care will be poor.

It costs money—four thousand to six thousand dollars a year per child, by government estimate. The temptation to cut corners is great. Parents alone can establish and maintain the standards they want. Unless you know what is best and insist on it, or unless you look for other solutions when you can't find the quality of care you want, day care won't be good care for your child today, or anyone else's children tomorrow.

Betty Vernon, Assistant Commissioner of Program Development in the New York City Agency for Child Development, and Maria Gravel and Hazel Osborn, who direct the unique Seton Hall Day Care Center at the New York Foundling Hospital, feel as strongly about this as we do. You will find all kinds and assortments of standards for day care. We have tried to list here the essentials, in order of importance, so it will be easy for you to judge a center by paying an observing visit and talking to the director and the particular staff member who will care for your child:

1. A trained and talented director who has a reputation for working easily with staff and whom you find easy to talk to.

2. A philosophy of child care that is congenial. For example, if you think children should be brought up to respect others for what they are, rather than for where they go to church, what kind of house they live in, or where they buy their clothes, you won't want a day care center where the staff and director make a point of telling you how affluent the children's parents are; how important their jobs are, etc.

If you think children grow their best by being allowed to explore, experiment, make mistakes, with grown-ups helping when they are needed, you won't choose a day care center where teachers see their role as entertaining and teaching children to do what they tell them to.

3. A positive attitude toward parents. The staff should be available at the beginning or end of the day to listen, report, or offer advice. Parents should be consulted and given a continuing, if informal, education in child development and care. The fewer children parents have, the fewer children they watched grow up in their childhood families, the more important is this aspect of day care.

4. Low staff turnover. A high percentage of trained staff and helpers who have worked in the center for upward of two years tells something about the character of the director and the program. It is also some assurance that your child will have the same teacher through the year.

5. Attitude toward children. A consistent approach to children throughout the staff, regardless of the individual's training. Look for men and women who are quiet, but responsive to children and flexible enough to be able to deal humorously with them, even when it's been a long day. As one director we talked to said, "You need teachers who are able to find more than one door to the house." I remember a spectacular teacher. When one two-year-old grabbed all the cookies at snacktime and the other children started screaming in unison, she calmly said, "Which two cookies do you want to keep?" Teachers have to avoid senseless confrontations and contests of will. The "I want them to know who's boss," approach gets nowhere.

6. Adequate staff. One to every four children under two. One to every six or seven children two and three.

7. Dry, sunny or well-lighted, spacious rooms with outside windows, where children can be separated by age and their momentary interests.

8. A closed-off room for babies, where they can nap, be fed, cuddled and played with, without being disturbed.

9. Adequate equipment for active and quiet play for each age group.

10. Reasonably sanitary facilities for cooking and cleaning up dishes, utensils. Good sanitary practice in diapering, toileting, etc. Adequate attention to children's physical safety. Fire protection.

11. A place to isolate children who become sick, until they can be picked up.

CHAPTER SIXTEEN

Q & A

Q. I am thinking about looking for a day care center for my baby. I am afraid I won't be satisfied at home all day, away from the work and the friends that are important to me. However, I don't want to sacrifice my baby to please myself for a few years. Can babies really develop as well in day care as they do at home?

A. Children develop best in the environment that best meets their needs. If all mothers were emotionally and financially secure and preferred spending most of their energy and attention on their children during the first years, children would probably be better off at home with them. However, whether we like it or not, these conditions do not exist. Today, many women have to work to support their children. Many others are neither emotionally nor intellectually suited to being alone with children all day in small apartments and homes, isolated from friends, family, and the social and mental stimulation they have been accustomed to.

There is no reason to assume that their children will suffer from being cared for by good mother substitutes, at home, or in day care centers. In fact, this kind of early experience may have certain advantages for children, particularly when the care is good and their experience at home is nourishing.

Several years ago pediatricians and psychologists made a study of two comparable groups of children in a southern town. One group was reared in a model day care center, from the early months, the other at home. The day care children—regardless of their economic or social backgrounds—were appreciably better developed, mentally and socially, at kindergarten age.

Psychologists from the University of Kentucky have recently made a pilot study of children from an assortment of *routine* day care centers. They found the day care children differed not at all—mentally or socially— from those brought up at home with mother.

Day care, when it is good, offers children a much greater variety of learning, play, and social experience than life with the average city or country mother does. Don't feel guilty about choosing day care when you are sure it is good.

Q. How can I be sure that even the best day care center is good for *my* child?

A. By your child's general appearance and behavior. If he is lively, alert, and willing—if not eager—to go each day, after the initial month or so of adjustment, you can assume that he is not suffering from the experience.

Telltale signs of discomfort are new fears; clinging and continuing to cry and mourn after you leave; appearing to be waiting for you anxiously each day when you come to pick him up, instead of being involved and busy; whining, tired, listless behavior at home; little progress or interest in trying new things.

Q. If my child seems to be unhappy should I take him out of day care?

A. I would consult with the director and the child's special teacher to see whether you can make any adjustments that will help. There may be other reasons for his anxiety. If he still seems miserable in day care, ask your pediatrician for advice.

Q. I can understand day care for toddlers, but I am afraid to enter my little baby. How could I tell that she would not suffer? I hardly know, yet, what is normal behavior for her, at two months.

A. The younger the child is, the more important it is to have a sensitive and responsive person taking care of him. It is also important for his caretaker or nurse to be with him more or less permanently so that she will get to know the baby's ways and needs and the baby will come to recognize and rely on her care. Even in my generation it was hard to get a nurse who would stay with a baby from birth until he went to school. Most working mothers had to leave their children with a succession of undistinguished baby tenders. In most instances the consequences were not too serious. I think that if you can find a day care center where the director has an established reputation and the workers are understanding, kind, and interested, your child will probably get the kind of attention he needs.

I spent a morning recently in a model day care center. I was particularly interested in seeing how the infants were cared for. There were five babies under seven months—three of whom had been in the center from the age of two months. Their "nurse" was a seventeen-year-old girl whom I would have been happy to leave my own children with. She rocked one boy in his carriage and chatted with me about all the babies. At the same time she had her eye on the three infants playing with their rattles and babbling quite intelligibly to each other on a playpen pad stretched out on the floor. Occasionally she caught the attention of one of them and said something specially to him.

I asked her why she was rocking the boy. "Mike just doesn't have sense enough to know when he's tired. He'd be awake all day if I didn't help him get his nap."

"Why shouldn't he stay awake?" I asked.

"He gets cranky and miserable if he doesn't sleep. I can tell when he's getting tired, and I rock him off."

A minute or so later Mike was asleep. Another baby arrived. Her mother put her on the playpen mat. A five-month-old playing quietly with his hands, stopped abruptly and went into spasms of delight when he saw her. She started jabbering away to him as if she couldn't wait to tell him all that had happened while they were apart.

The babies' nurse must have noticed my fascination at this scene. "Don't let anyone tell you that babies under three don't enjoy each other," she said. "Those two talk like that all day. Sheila's father calls her his 'gossip.' Isn't that cute?"

She diapered one, put on some special powder because, "He gets diaper rash easily. I can't see why. His mother is just as careful as I am," and so on.

I was with her for three hours as she rocked, fed, diapered, changed toys when babies got bored, showed a toddler who walked in how to comfort a crying one. She was happy, humorous, liked what she was doing, appreciated each child's special little self. It was obvious that she knew them all well and treated each one as an individual. I think that if one of those babies was yours you would be able to tell that he was well and prospering, and you would feel secure.

The great danger of putting children in day care—and the younger the child, of course, the greater the danger—is the effect of possible impersonal, sterile, faceless care. To develop into healthy human beings, children have to be able to attach themselves to familiar adults who almost magically, at first, respond to their helpless needs and feelings.

It is only against the background of this comfortable security that they develop the confidence that makes them move out into the world to explore and master.

Q. Sending a child to a day care center seems like putting him in an institution. I have read that institutional care is permanently harmful for young children. Is there the same danger in day care?

A. Institutions are harmful for little children if they fail to meet their emotional needs. Institutions used to emphasize physical care and good hygiene. As a result, babies were rarely fondled or touched. They were kept from getting dirty by being restrained alone in cribs and playpens. They were deprived of stimulation because of shortage of funds for staff and equipment. You are right. The resulting emotional deprivation was devastating to most children.

Current approved standards for good day care are designed to prevent a repetition of this kind of care. If you are interested in day care for your child, you can visit a number of centers and find one where children get personalized attention, stimulation, through toys and interaction with warm adults, and the good physical care that you try to give your child at home.

Q. Is there danger of infection spreading through a day care group?

A. Yes. The larger the enrollment, the greater the possibility that one child will bring in an infection that will be passed around. It is impossible to make a center one hundred per cent germproof and still provide the kind of atmosphere that will be emotionally healthy for the children. There has to be a compromise. If a worker stops to wash his hands every time he picks up a child, he'll soon stop picking up the children. Cuddling and playing will be sacrificed. Complete sterilization of diapers, clothes, dishes, and equipment is prohibitively expensive. It's impossible to keep toddlers from putting each other's toys in their mouths.

Brothers and sisters pass their colds around in their own homes. There have to be slip-ups. However, there are standards worked out by Health Departments that give reasonable protection. In the rare event of an epidemic, a day care center should close down until it can be brought under control.

Q. What alternatives would you suggest if a good day care center is not available?

A. In some localities women with experience and talent for taking care of babies and very small children are licensed to have one or two children at a time in their own homes. You might call your Town Hall and find out what department is in charge. Usually it is the Health Department or the Department of Child Welfare or Child Care. From the appropriate department, you can find out whether day care mothers are licensed, and see if there is a registry. Often women who provide day care in their homes advertise in local papers. Before you put your child in such a home, however, make sure the day care mother is certified so that you can count on minimal safety standards. Then satisfy yourself, by visiting and talking, that the "mother" will give the affectionate attention and variety of experiences you want your child to have.

I think it is very important to spend some time with the day care mother before you decide to leave your child with her, and after that I would recommend staying for several days, even if you think your baby is too young to notice the difference, until he has had time to adjust to a new person taking care of him. That way you will feel easier about the kind of care he will get, too.

Another arrangement is the co-operative day care group, put together by friends and neighbors who take turns caring for each other's children so that everyone in the group has some freedom to study, work part time, or do as she likes.

The danger in such arrangements, from what I have heard and seen, is that the members do not always agree, truly, about how children should be cared for, and are not necessarily able to be objective about children's behavior, especially when their own child is involved. The system also breaks down because members are not all equally conscientious about fulfilling their contracts.

For a co-op to be successful, members have to know each other well and trust each other implicitly.

Q. I worry sometimes about getting left behind in my career if I stay home until my children are in school all day. At the same time I want to be with them now. So much happens every day that I would hate to miss. Would they do better in day care where they would certainly have more children to play with and many more kinds of experience? I can't decide.

A. You should do what suits you best. If you enjoy being with your children and watching their daily progress as you describe, certainly they will benefit from your company and care. The children who gain most in day care are those who would not otherwise have much chance to be with children their own age, nor the space to play and things to do, nor the interested care of interested adults.

Q. Do you think children who start day care when they are very young lose out on the closeness and warmth of family life? Do they ever form really close family ties?

A. That depends on their parents. Mothers and fathers will have the same influence on their children during the evenings, nights, early mornings, and weekends when their children are with them that they would if they were home all day. In fact, many mothers have more fun with their children when they don't feel too hemmed in by them. If you are warm, affectionate, interested in what's happening to your child, good day care is not going to take that quality away. If you are the kind of parent who enjoys children when they are talking, working, studying, performing, more than you do at the baby stage, your child will probably benefit from the more infant-oriented kind of attention he can get from a good day care worker who has chosen what she is doing just because she likes babies best.

If you are worried that your child may develop deeper ties to the person who cares for him all day, you don't need to. Children, even on the kibbutzim in Israel, where they live away from parents from the first weeks, know perfectly well who their parents are, and identify with them first.

Good day care directors are aware of the danger of overinvolved workers creating problems for parents and children. If you ever have such fears, ask the day care director for advice.

Q. I don't feel that I am as responsive to my younger child, who has been in day care since he was a few months old, as I am to my little girl. I didn't go back to work until she was in nursery school.

A. Maybe you feel that you are shortchanging this child because you are not staying home with him. I don't think there is any reason why you should not be as sensitive to him as you were to your first child. Remember, each child is a different individual. Perhaps this one is a more self-sufficient person, and doesn't need as much from you. In any event, one of the values of a day care center is the opportunity it offers you to get an additional point of view on your child and how best to help him grow. Perhaps you should talk more often with your son's teacher or the center director. They may have some observations or advice that you will find helpful.

SPECIAL EDUCATION

About ten per cent of our children are physically, mentally, or emotionally handicapped, so that they cannot be properly educated in regular public school classes. Not long ago these children were sent to barren institutions, euphemistically known as "homes" or "schools," where they got sanitary care, at best, and cruel and inhuman treatment, at worst.

Helen Keller and others made the world gradually aware of the tragedy of wasted potential and unmet human needs in our casual treatment of the handicapped. More enlightened attitudes have led to widespread changes in the education, training, and care of the retarded, the crippled, the deaf, blind, emotionally ill, and children with perceptual problems that interfere with learning.

Those of us who see the progress such children can make in overcoming or compensating for their weaknesses know the talents and abilities that may lie buried beneath the handicaps. We recognize that education for the handicapped, even more than for the child with normal endowment, is of crucial importance.

The right of the handicapped to education and training that will develop, to the fullest, the abilities they have so that they may live as independent and satisfying lives as possible has been established in our courts. Most states and local governments allocate funds for special education. Where the population of handicapped children is large enough special classes or schools are often incorporated into the public school system. Where no public school facilities are available, the school district or county, with state aid, pays for special education in approved schools. In New York State, parents are allowed two thousand dollars a year for special education in approved private schools when parents have established that appropriate resources are not available in the regular public schools of their community.

The largest group of children who need special education are the retarded. They represent two or three per cent of the population. The physically handicapped are another large group, some of whom cannot get along in the public schools. Special education is also needed for children with impaired hearing or vision, emotional problems, and learning disorders, including minimal brain damage, central language impairment, perceptual and motor dysfunction, minimal brain dysfunction, and dyslexia.

All parents want their children to live as normal and happy and full lives as it is possible for them to provide. The parents' natural hopes, however, sometimes make it hard to do what's best for the child who is not like the others. It is easier for us always to believe that a child is all right, or soon will be, if he is properly cared for, properly taught, and tries hard. But the facts do not always support such hopes and wishes. When parents, in the face of expert advice to the contrary, insist that their children can be and do and become what all the scientific skill and human devotion in the world cannot accomplish, it only adds to the frustration and isolation of the handicapped child and the sorrow of the parents.

I think of a small child I used to know. Her mother had contracted rubella in the first weeks of her pregnancy and this little girl was born almost totally deaf, as a result. This was established when she was a very young baby. Nevertheless, when she was two and a half and still did not talk, her mother insisted that she could talk as well as I could, if she were not so contrary.

The mother was not cruel at all. It was her pathetic way of trying to make her little girl O.K. Fortunately, this child was healthy and intelligent. With good training she learned to communicate, first with sign language and later by talking. She understands. She can communicate. She is learning. She will have a good life. But, if her mother had not given up her fantasy version of what was going on, her daughter would still be locked in the frustrating bind of not being able to get the tools that have allowed her to find her way into the hearing, speaking, reading, writing world.

Specialists in the education and training of handicapped children have the same goal that parents have: to make life as normal as the child's limitations will allow. It is impossible to predict with absolute certainty the outer limits of any human being's capacities. Too many imponderables, such as will, motivation, unforeseeable developmental changes, enter in to confound the best diagnostician. However, an expert prognosis, based on the child's history, thorough testing and examination, is still the soundest basis for planning his education. A child's performance may exceed our fondest hopes, and nothing is lost. But, when expert advice is ignored, and the child is subjected to educational demands that he cannot possibly meet, the inevitable discouragement and frustration that follow may keep him from ever realizing his potential.

In the interest of childhood as usual, we try to keep handicapped children in school with their peers wherever possible. Being with regular children, day in, day out, seeing them as models of the way things are supposed to be, helps the handicapped child try to be as much like them and do as much as they do. Even when he can't keep up, their presence allows him to enjoy aspects of life that would otherwise be shut off for him. Being with his age group makes him one with them in friendship—most important of all—and in all aspects of experience that he shares with them. It keeps him from the singular isolation of being in the world, but not of the world.

Children whose handicaps do not interfere with learning can get along well in regular classrooms. Schools have made great advances in adapting to their special needs.

For example, children who cannot walk alone, can go to school in buses equipped to load and unload them in their wheel chairs. They may not be able to do everything other children can. They may not be able to go to the board, read out loud, take part in class discussion. They usually can't take gym. But there may also be some things they can do that others cannot. They may be better students. They may draw funnier cartoons; write better poems or stories; be better coaches in sports; be able to referee games.

They often have to call on others for help. If they can't write clearly, they may need someone to help get their homework down on paper. Friends may assist by getting their food in the cafeteria; looking up books in the library; running errands; picking up dropped objects; helping with coats. There are benefits for helpers and helped. Teachers recognize what the helper learns about responsibility and understanding and the meaning of friendship; and what the helped gains from living in the "real" world.

When handicaps prevent children from attending regular classes all day long they may still be able to get something out of going part time. A number of children whom I work with go to regular neighborhood schools with their friends part or most of the time. Some of them have very poor vision. Some have seriously impaired hearing. Nevertheless, with glasses or hearing aids, and the co-operation of their teachers—who make sure they are sitting where they can get most, if not all, of what is going on—they keep up. The class atmosphere and their interest in being participants make them try harder. Extra tutoring from special teachers in the system helps them with whatever they may miss in class.

When the others are at gym or shop or doing something else that they couldn't enjoy, they have special work. It might be corrective drill for a particular learning disability; speech therapy; physiotherapy; training in sign or lip reading; practice in reading or typing in Braille; or review of regular classroom work.

Even among children who are so handicapped that they cannot usually get along at all in regular classes during their early years, there are some who may eventually be able to make it in the world of their peers. Children with the kinds of learning and/or behavior patterns that—for want of more exact definition—are referred to as minimal brain damage or dysfunction (two separate and distinct entities), or perceptual and motor dysfunction, or dyslexia are examples that come to mind.

We hate to take a child out of the world of his age-mates completely when it looks as if he would eventually be able to cope with his problem well enough to get along in a regular school. We don't want him to lose touch with his peers. We want him to remain familiar with the routines and have the stimulation of the normal school day as well as the fun and games that go with it. Therefore, when we can, we try to hold the special classes such children require within the walls of the regular school. This system operates in several schools in New York City. As the children improve and their teachers think they are almost up to grade level in performance, they begin to spend part of a day once a week, to start, and then gradually longer periods, in a regular class at their level in the same building. If they can't make it on the first try, no harm is done. The teacher simply decides to wait a little longer and the child goes back to his special class, usually more determined than before to make it on the next try. If he gets along all right, he eventually switches to the regular class full time. Then at the beginning of the next school year he goes to his neighborhood school as a student with no stigma.

If he had to enter his neighborhood elementary school for his trial period, this smooth transition would not be possible. In that case, if he failed, he'd be stamped for the rest of his life there, even though he succeeded in adjusting on the second try. His return to his special school would be a defeat, too.

Unfortunately, most small town and rural systems cannot support special education for the handicapped. If you live in a school district where this is true, you should turn to the school supervisor's office for guidance about where to apply for help in securing appropriate special education for your child.

Sometimes a county or a regional district provides special education in one school and transportation for all the children in the area who need it.

When there are no day schools available, there are usually state boarding schools in different sections of the state that provide education for the handicapped. If there is no public facility in your community, your state and local district may assume financial responsibility for the child's education in a private school, or provide for a visiting teacher in the home. You can find out from the superintendent of schools in your town or county how to qualify for assistance and what private schools are certified for state aid. Your doctor will probably recommend the schools he feels are most suitable for your needs. Visit those you are considering, once or twice, so that you can judge the quality of the education and training, the general care, and the program of activities.

You should also find out about the training and experience of the supervisors and teachers to be sure that they can give the kind of education and training your child needs. I would also talk to other parents of past and present students to satisfy yourself that the environment is a healthy, happy one, and the school is successful in returning those who have the potential to regular life.

Parents rarely choose to send children away to school, particularly when they are little. It is not simply that they associate boarding schools with the old custom of putting children away—hiding them from the stares of the community; but also because of parents' normal desire to watch over the care and progress of children during the years when they are so dependent and close to you.

Normal, natural, and understandable as this impulse is, it is not always wise for the seriously handicapped child's own future, or for the other children in the family.

I can remember a little boy who did not hear. His parents did their very best for him, but they still were unable to decide whether he disobeyed because he didn't understand or because he was spoiled. They weren't very sure about how much to frustrate him and how much spoiling was permissible, even so. As a result, this four-year-old was not learning how to get along in the world, how to talk, or how to learn. He was also taking so much of his parents' time and attention that his older sister and younger brother were beginning to act truly deprived. When I finally persuaded Jonathan's parents to send him to a boarding school for the deaf they were just about as skeptical as they could be. I still don't know why they followed my advice, but they did. Every Monday morning at six they drove three hours to school and as early as possible on Friday afternoon they drove three hours to get him and three hours more to bring him home. At first, the whole weekend was one long trauma. Jonathan cried when they got him; made life hell all the time he was home; and cried all the way back.

Then, after a month or so, he began to settle down. He greeted them rather casually when they came, and ran off to his friends without saying good-by when they left him. He's been in the school six months now. He knows how to fit into the family like the other children. He often brings school friends home, or joins friends from school during vacations. He has developed a real life within the family, and a life of his own, independent of the family—which is the normal thing for a boy going on five.

Parents all want their children to be able to live like everyone else. If that cannot be possible, try to face it. There is nothing worse for any human being than isolation from others. If your child is not and cannot be an accepted member of his natural peer group, spare him the pain of being an outsider. Find an environment where he can adapt. In a community where grown-ups understand and care for him, the children play together as equals, and the program is one he can enjoy and learn from, a child will progress. As a misfit who spends his days in uncomprehending isolation, and the rest of the time at home alone he will stand still, or regress.

This issue arises most particularly with children who cannot reasonably be expected to make much improvement under any circumstances. Often parents hesitate to follow professional advice to send their retarded children to boarding schools. They have seen these children improve from infancy to some extent, and they are convinced that they are just slower at learning than other children, but will catch up eventually. They believe that if they are patient, loving, and persistent in teaching, the child will catch up. They fear that he will regress without them. They cannot accept the fact that constitutional factors prevent him from developing beyond a certain level.

There are different degrees of retardation. Some children are so mildly retarded that they can eventually get along in routine jobs and become independent and self-supporting. If a child's IQ is 75 or over he will be able to function at the twelve-year level, if he is properly trained. A child with an IQ of 50 will never progress beyond the level of an eight-year-old. While he may learn to take care of himself in a protected environment, he will probably not be able to get along on his own.

Severely retarded children often cannot learn to take care of themselves and must, of necessity, be confined at home or in an institution for life.

If a child has the potential for being independent, the parent must decide what environment is best for him. The good boarding school has some definite advantages. Children have companionship. They have more practice learning tasks that they can master. They are learning the same things the other children are learning instead of being special and alone. Under these circumstances many children make better progress than they would at home.

Children are infinitely adaptable, as anyone who is used to watching great numbers of sick and handicapped children has to notice. They can make do in amazing ways with whatever they have. But no human child survives very well without touching and being touched; without friendly contact at meals and in all the activities that children normally share with their peers and teachers and families. When a family can offer this experience and the community can supply the special education needed, children can prosper at home. If the training and opportunities for companionship are not possible at home, it is harmful and sentimental, in my opinion, not to look for a suitable boarding school.

When you weigh what's best for your child consider, also, his nature and your own. Some individuals have more patience, more tolerance for frustration, greater ability to accept differences in others—whether children or adults. These qualities make it easier to work with children who are retarded or handicapped. No amount of devotion and love for a child gives one these temperamental qualities when they aren't there.

Some children have qualities of personality that make it easier for them to get along with their handicaps in the community. A child, for example, who is sunny, cheerful, and affectionate invites help and friendship. The child who is shy and withdrawn is easy to ignore.

Certain combinations of parent and child would never make it well together under optimal conditions. Certain others make a good working team whether the going is rough or smooth. Try to face yourselves honestly. Whatever the opportunities in your community for care, treatment, education, training, and companionship, there is no valid reason for keeping a child with you unless you are congenial and compatible, and his brothers and sisters get along with him and want him home. If a child is the focus of family tension, your obligation is to find an environment for him in which he can develop best.

The child's nature—his temperamental qualities— should also help dictate the corrective measures that are taken to help him. There are two approaches to education and rehabilitation of the handicapped. One group of educators believes in overcoming weakness and the other concentrates on working from strength. Supporters of the first approach believe, for example, that a child born with no usable hearing should be encouraged from the beginning to learn to speak. Those who believe in the second approach would advise parents to communicate from early infancy in sign language.

Let us say the problem is a learning disability that prevents a child from organizing the printed word in the right sequence in order to be able to read. The first group would drill the child with specific tasks in an effort to train him out of his disability. The second group would teach the child orally.

Those who believe in the direct approach—attacking a particular weakness to overcome it—believe that this method mobilizes strengths that would otherwise remain undeveloped and useless.

Those who believe in the roundabout route think it produces practical results faster and thus encourages the child to work directly on overcoming his weakness when he is older.

If you have a handicapped child, you will want to read a good deal more about education and rehabilitation; and about ways of handling your child's specific difficulty. However, I think it is important, in evaluating a school, or a form of treatment, or a child's progress in treatment to consider how well a given method works for him. Flexibility is invaluable in dealing with children under any circumstances. It is especially valuable when children have handicapping problems of any kind. There is merit in encouraging them to overcome their problems, to develop their abilities, and function to the utmost. But there are times and circumstances when this approach is definitely unrewarding, if not counterproductive.

There are certain children who are by temperament so easily discouraged or so sensitive, that they might be lost forever if they had to learn to walk with braces. However, they could achieve great mobility if they could use wheel chairs. There are deaf children who would be starved emotionally if they could not communicate with parents and siblings fluently in sign for the long years until they could be taught lip reading and speech.

You as a parent have to be open to whatever approach is recommended. You also have the responsibility to see for yourself how it is working in practice; whether the child is working happily with it, has become tired and passive, or is definitely giving up. If things are not going well perhaps it might be time for you to discuss a change in treatment or training. The most useful way of treating the handicapped is the most flexible way; the way that draws on every approach that is practiced in order to find the methods that work best for your child from day to day.

YOUR VALUES OR THEIRS?

Decent behavior, ethical principles may seem strange
subjects for a book about helping children in school.
They would have been in the days when children who
got along in school ordinarily grew up to become independent, responsible adults.

Today a visible minority of promising young people
who fall or drift into anti-social or self-destructive behavior makes parents uneasy.

What has changed? Adolescents—grown up, but dependent; powerful, but untried; desperately trying to
prove they're free of their parents, but not really feeling
that way—lean heavily on their peers for support. The
more anti-adult or far out the demands of the peer
group, the greater their lure. Adult values seem to sym-
bolize baby values. Rebellion, on the other hand, looks
like independence.

Peer pressures are strongest when social pressures
are weakest. School children have always cheated. Politics has always been corrupt. Businessmen have always
had two sets of values—one for the market, another for
the home. Somehow, nevertheless, honesty, the golden
rule, the brotherhood of man, equality of opportunity

were ideals you could talk about without smirking. After the Vietnam war and the saga of Watergate it is not so easy. The ideals we are supposed to live by have been dishonored at the very top levels of government, where grown-ups as well as children traditionally look for models, and no one has escaped exposure to the fall. The broken veterans, the GI orphans, the child beggars and whores of Vietnam, the droning voices of the plumbers and extortioners in high places have come to every home.

Sensitive teen-agers, looking for causes to enlist in, and daring, concerned, humane men and women to pattern their lives by, react with cynicism and despair. If we don't mean what we say, if honesty is not the best policy, if the bad guys win, what's the use? Forget it. Forget what THEY say. Forget study. Forget careers. Drop out. Goof off. Forget the mess with pills, and/or drugs, and/or alcohol.

Recently, rising enrollments in professional schools, a growing parade of dropouts returning to school, and a marked decline in drug use have led some to hope that disaffection, alienation, and the drug culture and life styles that went with them, were losing their hold.

Even at the crest of the nihilist wave, however, many resisted. Why did they hold out? Why is the wave ebbing, if it is? The decline in drug use may be explained, as one young patient explained it to me: "When you see enough of your friends turn into vegetables, you begin to think twice."

Young people who have been there and back may be learning that self-destruction and emptiness are not the only, nor the best ways to escape a world you don't like. They may be deciding to take responsibility for making the kinds of lives they want.

Obviously, no magic formula can explain any social phenomenon, or individual choice. Parents, grandparents, neighborhoods, teachers, school, the nature of the individual are all influential. Something as ephemeral as chance can sometimes be decisive—chance that puts one child at the wrong place at the wrong time and another at the right place at the crucial moment; chance that makes one child so sure of wanting to be a lawyer at thirteen that no group and no lure could deflect him; chance that one teacher attracts one lost child and turns him around at just the right moment.

From my own experience with the children in our study—all of whom are in or past the "dangerous" age now—children who get to adolescence on speaking terms with their parents are way ahead.

Conversation between teen-agers and their parents may sound like a trivial bit of evidence to hang a prediction on, but it tells a great deal about the quality of family life. It tells how children feel about their parents and how they feel about themselves and these are the factors that decide what they do with themselves in their teens.

I'm not talking about "Pass the bread," "Where's my notebook?" "Did you see that fumble?" "This girl has the neatest clothes. I want . . ." "I'm going to Charley's" kind of bulletins. I mean communication that says something about the people who are talking—who they are, what they feel, what they want for themselves and each other, what they believe in, what worries them, what upsets them, and what makes them happy. This kind of talk tells that the family is a going institution; a haven where people can be themselves, express themselves, expose themselves, knowing that they will get the help or appreciation, or laughs or sympathy, they expect, and won't be put down, laughed at, ignored, or hurt.

It is the kind of dialogue that can take place only in an atmosphere of mutual respect, trust, and enjoyment. Where this exists, children have room to move around in. Because they feel free to confess their doubts, ask advice, make mistakes, and try on responsibility as they grow, they don't have the interior pressure to blast off that makes them so susceptible to the blandishments of their peers.

Many different kinds of parents create this kind of open, comfortable family. It requires a kind of compassionate view of the human condition, acceptance of the tentative nature of progress, and a kind of basic satisfaction with one's own modest place in the world.

These are the qualities that allow parents to accept their children and enjoy watching and helping them grow in their own ways, instead of trying to turn them into someone else. People who possess these qualities do not use their children to buck up their own egos. They don't punish them for not satisfying their needs. They don't need their children for their own fulfillment, so they can comfort, correct, encourage, praise, please, amuse as necessary—communicating, almost by osmosis, their own decent, workable attitude toward life.

Who does it? No one, of course, all the time. We can only try. Children are generous. They allow lots of backsliding; have an eerie way of picking up the spirit of parents' ways; and give lots of credit for good intentions.

One holiday when I was four or five I was walking through New York's Central Park with my mother and sister on the way to the carousel or zoo, I suppose. A car full of very happy black people singing at the top of their lungs drove by. My mother stopped walking and with a really bitter expression on her face said, "They ride and we walk."

As early as I can remember I knew that every child was as deserving of respect, care, and help as every other. My mother said it and she lived it. We knew from the stories she brought home from school and her insistence that all second-graders—black, white, rich, and poor—learn to read before they left her.

Living in the middle class world of that time, the popular, racist stereotype of the carefree, high-living, easygoing colored people had influenced her thinking, willy-nilly. On that morning—tired and overburdened as she was—self-pity must have momentarily conquered reason. Even though what she said puzzled me, I didn't stop believing in her. That rare transgression may have helped teach me that people are only human. You may not be able to live up to your ideals all the time, but having ideals helps your children have some too.

There has been a good deal of nonsense written lately about the terrible influence of parental hypocrisy on juvenile manners and morals. Looking for loopholes in the income tax law—a perfectly legal practice—is a favorite example.

I can't really believe that a generation brought up with television and radio in today's world is going to throw ethics to the winds and take to drink and drugs because their parents drive faster than the speed limit, shove kids under subway turnstiles when they can, and try to avoid parking fines.

Children can tell inconsequential lies from the total absence of any dependable integrated set of values in their parents. They have to learn the difference for survival. Parents who project an image of absolute infallibility intimidate children, who can't imagine ever being able to satisfy their parents' lofty expectations. In fact, parents who are too good make their children feel so inferior that they often give up trying to meet parental standards.

Parents who are too good keep their children from developing judgment about when to be truthful, when to be still, and when to compromise.

Everyone has to learn when the social lie is appropriate, when incidental carelessness is acceptable, when to violate rules on purpose, in order to get along peaceably.

"Oh, what a pretty dress," you say to John's friend, Patsy. Later your son John says, "But, Ma, you know you hate yellow."

And you say, "I do, but Patsy doesn't. Why make her feel bad?"

You say, "Let's cross now." And your five-year-old says, "But you said not to cross when the light's red."

And you say, "Right, you shouldn't. But I'm with you and I can see nothing is coming. When you're older you can do the same thing."

You're on a plane. Gretchen, a self-righteous nine, says, "You told the lady that Sean is five, but he is six, Daddy. You know that."

"Yes, Gretchen," you explain, "but I think this airline is getting enough from this family today. Sean's not a very big six."

Ethics reflect what we feel about people. They're not much use in the abstract. They are practiced on people. If we are kind, honest, helpful, understanding with each other and our friends, kids can hardly get the idea that it's O.K. to cheat and lie and steal when it is convenient. If we manage to work with some satisfaction and success, they won't get the idea that there's no use trying to get into the rat race. If we make clear our disapproval of government when it violates its own, or our own standards of humane behavior, our children won't get the idea that the country is so hopeless they have to drop out.

Children absorb our values as automatically as they learn to walk and talk, and probably even before. What we believe is so important to them that the negativistic children—those who don't get along with their parents—invariably violate the very values their parents put first. If their parents are scrupulously neat, they are slobs. If their parents are painfully honest, they lie and cheat, and so on. Children who have amiable relationships with their parents aren't quite as scrupulous about honoring your ideals as the rebels are in rejecting them, but you can be sure that what you say and do sticks, and is weighed in the balance when they have to decide how to act.

Nevertheless, the goodness of parents and children has a lot to prevail against these days. There was a time when schools and teachers could be counted on to support parents' efforts to show and tell children right ways from wrong ones. Today, schools are often counterinfluences.

When I was a resident one of the internes I supervised blandly tore up his mistaken diagnosis and prepared a predated correct one after listening to the chief of the service analyze the case on rounds. Devotion to truth is essential to the practice of scientific medicine. It was hard for me, at that time, to believe that a good mark was so important to that brand-new doctor that truth became totally expendable.

That is the first time I remember being aware of what competition, as a motivating force, does to an individual's integrity and, indirectly, to the values of society. Students who are judged by marks and rank are encouraged to give answers, rather than to think, question, and explore. They are also tempted to cheat rather than learn or value the goals of their study—in this case, good medicine.

The so-called *best* academic high schools tax students' integrity to the limit. Even the strongest kids need group approval. Your influence may prevent cheating, but it may not. Whether a teen-ager holds on to what he believes in may rest on the friends he goes to school with. I know a boy who found friends who shared his view that competition was for the birds. They actually made fun of the obsession with marks that gripped the student body. They may not have had much clout with the majority, but they provided enough mutual support to keep each other going.

Under the best circumstances teen-agers have lapses from the ethical and social values you have tried to give them. If you are prepared, you may be able to keep backsliding from getting serious.

If you suspect trouble, say so.

Don't drop hints that you *feel* something is wrong. Don't temporize. Don't pussyfoot. Find out all you can. Then talk about it. I say *talk*.

Hysterical screaming, loud noises, dangerous accusations, and violent recriminations are more likely to produce alienation than reform. If there is trouble, make the least of it.

If you get along with your child and have his confidence, don't risk losing it. If you do, you will lose your influence and usefulness to him when he may need you most.

The approach I suggested using when a child needs

help in school will be much more successful. First, be sure that your expectations are not excessive and that there really is trouble.

If you know there is a real problem, give the child a chance to talk about it. You will get more clues about how to help than you will if you shut him up by over-reacting. That will simply teach him to learn better ways to conceal his bad practices.

Too many questions, at machine gun speed, sound just like attacks. When you ask a question, be sure to wait for an answer and then listen to it.

If the problem is drugs, you are likely to hear the familiar bromide, "Don't worry. I'm perfectly able to take it or leave it. Don't you think I know what I'm doing? I just want to see what they're like. It's part of our generation's experience."

Don't buy that. Remind your child with cool clarity of the boys or girls whom you both know who said those very words before they went under. You may get pooh-poohed, but you will be heard. The memory of your calmly spoken facts may then become a restraining influence at a crucial moment.

Let the parents of your child's friends know what's going on. Alert your child's school—choosing the teacher or administrator you know best and respect the most. The more responsible members of the community know that drugs are available, the more likelihood there will be that an effective program for drug control will be set up. You can see that it is, of course, by taking an active role in getting a program started.

When your children are small and have trouble making friends, or learning their lessons, or behaving properly in class, you do all you can to get them over their trouble. You try to find out what's behind it. You give the help, encouragement, support, or discipline that you think is needed. You watch and wait. You change your tactics when you don't see progress. But at some point you must say to yourself, "I've done all I can or should. He knows what he's doing. He knows what he should be doing. It's up to him." You recognize that part of being a parent is knowing when to give up your responsibility for your child so that he can learn to become responsible for himself.

This is a terribly hard decision to make, particularly when a child may be facing real danger, but it is wise. If you do it in a way that leaves the door open for the child to come back to you when he feels unsure or threatened, it may be the very move that helps him turn the corner to maturity.

INDEX